I shall pass through this world but once. Any good therefore that I can do or any kindness that I can show to any human being, let me do it now. Let me not defer or neglect it for I shall not pass this way again.

EX LIBRIS

WENDY S. WEINGER

Stepparenting

Stepparenting

Jean Rosenbaum, M.D.
and
Veryl Rosenbaum, Psa.

Ink Drawings by Judith Clancy Johns

CHANDLER & SHARP PUBLISHERS, INC.
Corte Madera, California

To Ara Martin, a fine man and our own Step Dad

Library of Congress Cataloging in Publication Data

Rosenbaum, Jean.

    Stepparenting.

    Bibliography: p.

    1. Stepparents.   I. Rosenbaum, Veryl, joint author.   II. Title.

HQ777.7.R67   301.42'72'0431   77-22070

ISBN 0-88316-530-9

Copyright © 1977 by Chandler & Sharp Publishers, Inc.
All rights reserved.
Library of Congress Catalog Card Number 77-22070

International Standard Book Number 0-88316-530-9

Printed in the United States of America.

Book designed by Joe Roter

Editor: Rudite J. Emir

Composition by Hansen & Associates Graphics

Contents

Introduction

The Stepchild Syndrome

The Henderson family is driving toward a picnic site. The parents look happy, expecting a pleasant afternoon. The two children in the back seat, Joan, five, and Andrew, eight, look glum. Between bouts of bickering they throw hateful glances at Mrs. Henderson, their stepmother. What's going on here? Picnics are supposed to be *fun*! Finally, Mrs. Henderson tells Andrew to stop teasing his sister, and Andrew, turning red, yells, "You can't tell me what to do—you're not my Mom!" Joan starts to cry, Mrs. Henderson feels defeated, and the father feels helpless.

This particular scene in its various guises is repeated thousands of times a day in homes across America. Our country has the highest divorce and remarriage rate in the world. In fact, on the average, the incidence of broken marriages is one out of every two, but the rate jumps even higher among those who marry young and have children.

The wars have also left their mark by creating large numbers of new families, and with the subsequent divorces, have left us with an enormous population of stepchildren who have very special problems to deal with besides the already difficult task of growing up. If this situation does not exist in your family, then for certain it must among some of your friends.

Let's first consider the children of divorced parents. Divorce does not have to leave an emotional scar on a child's personality. It is much more honest to divorce your spouse if there is no possibility of making a working marriage than it is to stay together for the sake of the children. When such children do grow up, they feel contempt for the parents who stayed together in hate and misery for "their sakes." How does it benefit children to grow up in such an atmosphere? And implicit in this arrangement is, "I have sacrificed my life for my children; they owe me something now." A whole cycle of resentment and guilt is started into motion with that decision. Children usually do not like divorce, but they can accept it and understand it if told that the parents love them and always will. It is bad for *everyone*, however, to live in an unhappy home, especially one without love between adults.

Children can live with divorce even more easily if the parents have the wisdom to refrain from making a child choose sides, and if they refrain from telling awful stories about each other and generally behaving like three-year-olds. Children need a model of adult love to identify with, or they will carry a model of hate into their own marriages.

All stepchildren, of course, are not the products of divorce. The death of one parent is quite devastating to the children. Just when they need the surviving parent most, they discover that that person is mourning too. Because of their rich fantasy life, children often feel responsible for the parent's death. Fantasies will be especially vivid if the children have had daydreams of anger and destruction toward a parent for frustrating them in the process of helping them grow up. These feelings *must* be talked about in order for growth to continue.

The childhood years are emotionally strenuous for

everyone. It takes at least eighteen years to complete the process physically, and sometimes even longer psychologically. All parents are aware of the awesome responsibility of rearing a family. Their challenge is to give their children love, care, discipline, a sense of worth, a figure to identify with, education, principles, and strength to face the world. That's an enormous undertaking even if done only in a minimal way.

When this job is complete, the young adult should be able to leave home and be an independent person, physically and emotionally. Each child passes through the parents' life and leaves to make his or her own way. Parents who expect gratitude, undying love, and thanks for their long years of work are in for a shock. Children do not owe their parents anything. It's the parents' responsibility to do their job if they bring children into the world.

Such is the normal load we carry with offspring. Many complications can occur in rearing children in the usual family; but if you have stepchildren, you are no doubt very aware of the additional psychological forces that develop when people remarry and form a new family.

Stepparenting does not have to be destructive to anyone. As a matter of fact, it can be a wonderful new opportunity for personality expansion in a child.

Everyone who remarries has the usual difficulties of setting up a new home and of adjusting to another person's life style and habits. Adjustment in a second marriage is smoother in the sense that at least one party has gone through the process once before; but it is more difficult, on the other hand, because children may be present from the beginning. We think it's helpful if the courtship is at least six months long in order to allow the stepparent and children to develop some positive feelings for each other. For example, you can try picnics, movies, and walks with the children, first with both parents, and then separately. The object is the same as that of Anna, the new teacher in "The King and I": "Getting to Know You."

If the transition is not smooth, the shock of being suddenly thrust into a new position is too great—on both sides. The stepparent has a big job ahead.

All children who must accept a new mother or father because of divorce or death would simply rather not do it. In a child's mind and heart he or she has only one mother and one father, no matter how unpleasant the lost parent may have been. No matter if the parent is alive or dead, thousands of miles away, institutionalized, or living a mile away—there is still only the original pair in the child's thoughts.

By the same token, it doesn't matter how kind and loving and understanding the stepparent is, he or she is thought of as an intruder into the children's lives. If the remarriage happens after a divorce, children always have a fantasy that someday Mom and Dad will get back together again. Even if the first marriage was a disastrous affair with yelling and fighting, the fantasy remains. It's human nature to dislike change, even in bad situations. These facts must be kept in mind in order truly to understand the dilemma of stepchildren.

Before the second marriage, children usually have a period that they spend alone with one parent. They enjoy having the attention of the parent without having to share it with another adult. This point is important to understand. Children feel a normal frustration in family life. Mother and father have (or should have) something special together in which children are not included. Children try to get between parents to get some of that special attention. They are normal triangle-makers and instinctive manipulators. They are frustrated when they cannot succeed, and, ideally, this frustration pushes them to form their own relationships in life. The struggle may be somewhat unpleasant for all parties in the triangle, but the frustration resulting from it is a vital force in a child's growth. Thus, if the child has had the parent alone for any length of time, the youngster feels that the stepparent is again taking something away rather than adding something good to his or her life.

Keeping the "one set of parents" in mind, imagine how difficult it must be for stepchildren to deal with their feelings if they happen to *like* the new parent! Simultaneous like-dislike is a confusing emotion. Little ones have a hard time grasping the fact that a person is capable of loving many people. They experience guilt if they have positive feelings toward their stepparents. They feel disloyal to the original parent, and so they try to "unlike" the stepparent, usually by being mean and rude and forcing the new parent into the role of "the mean witch" or "horrible monster." Then they can say, "See? I really don't like that person anyway—just my real Mom (Dad)."

That is the stepchild's own special problem. How can you deal with this emotional mechanism? The first step is to develop a thick skin and try to separate your stepchildren's turmoil of feelings from your own. Try not to take their mean remarks personally. Encourage them to talk out, play out, or draw out what they are really experiencing underneath. Allow children to speak openly about their contradictory feelings so that they do not have to carry the burden alone. "You're not my real mother" can be handled thus: "No, I know I'm not. You have two Moms (Dads). Your real one and a second one—me. I can't be the real one; but as myself, I love you and care about you and want you to be happy. Even if I'm not your *real* Mom, I still want to help you grow up."

Let the children know that feeling angry and cheated is all right, that it doesn't hurt your feelings, that you understand they'd like their parents to be together again. Reality must be faced by saying, "I know you want them together again; it's *normal* to want this; but we are married now."

Children also have little concept of leaving home someday and starting their own families. They think everything will remain static. Some parents forget this too. Keep the perspective of time and growth in mind. As a stepparent you may expect gratitude: "I took over these children, supported them, looked after them, loved them and cared for them, and they don't care!" Too bad. Children are not a very thankful bunch, whether they are your own or someone else's. So do not expect anything in return for your parenting. It's your job to understand and help them, not vice versa. You will have to carry the knowledge within your own heart that you made every attempt to help a confused child become a happier, more accepting person.

Maybe, and just maybe, many years later when that child is an adult and is happily married as a result of your painful efforts, he or she will return with a feeling of friendship and a small thank-you.

PART **I**

*CONTEMPLATING
STEPPARENTING*

Chapter **1**

Changes in the Family

If you are about to become a stepparent, realize that the family you are joining has a complicated history. You may be entering into a new family situation with children of your own. Whatever the mix might be—a single woman marrying a man with custody of his children, a mother with two of her own marrying a man with occasionally visiting offspring, or a child-free couple whose children from a previous marriage reappear on the doorstep after an absence of five years—whatever the mix, the situation is complex.

Such family mixes prevail in present-day society as a result of our casual mating and divorce habits, increases in fatal accidents and suicides, parental abandonment, and recent war deaths. We also have a new social phenomenon of women opting to stay single while bearing children. This decision can be reversed when the mother falls in love, and the child then has an instant father. The divorce rate continues to climb, but the majority of people, whether single through catastrophe or divorce, long to establish another deep relationship with and commitment to another.

3

Whatever the circumstances that leave us with millions of stepparents, new stepparents have one of the most demanding, exasperating, but potentially rewarding jobs of parenting ahead of them.

Let us examine the past history of children and adults who have been emotionally traumatized by a family breakdown and the eventual disruption caused by one parent leaving.

SURVIVING DIVORCE OR DEATH

Divorce rarely occurs abruptly. Because humans have the unique emotional attributes of hope, trust, motivation, and love, when marital difficulties arise, they will first choose to stay married to try to solve their problems. As our divorce statistics show, a great many fail. In the meantime the children are witness to a lot of arguing, beating (sometimes of them), loud, angry shouting, and plenty of adult tears. The situation can only be very stressful.

Unhappy adults tend to neglect or even to exploit their children's emotional needs. Though the parents may love their children, the couple are usually drained by the stresses of their marital battles.

Randy, ten, and his little sister Sue, six, were referred to our clinic by their pediatrician. The boy suffered from tension headaches and the girl from stomachaches. Both symptoms appeared regularly on Monday mornings and were severe enough to keep the children out of school. Both parents worked, so the usual scramble of Monday mornings was compounded by the necessity of hiring a baby-sitter or of one parent staying home to care for the whiney children.

Our clinic is a cheerful place, decorated to alleviate patient's fears. Comfortable couches, rather than the standard plastic modern, tables and chairs for children, and lots of half-broken toys usually manage to put everyone at ease. However, when this tense family came to the clinic, everyone was too nervous and upset even to sit down. Mom, Dad, Randy, and Sue all came into the consultation room together. The parents listed their children's ills, not just headaches and stomach problems, but also their clinging ways and general irritability. Both adults discussed "them" as if they were just bad children without names who actually enjoyed getting sick and causing parental inconvenience.

The parents were asked to wait in the reception room while we talked with the children. When they left, Sue became weepy, Randy put a defensive arm around her shoulder, as though in the course of his life he had become a mini-parent with the responsibility of comforting her. This behavior is not usual for children in a nonthreatening atmosphere with caring and warm therapists. We reassured them that their parents were just in the next room and we would only talk for a few minutes.

Randy knew why they both got sick on Mondays. He said all weekend his Mom and Dad had bad fights, with both screaming that they were going to leave. "Lots of times, Dad runs out the door and takes off in the car. That leaves me to take care of Suzy, 'cause Mom goes to bed," said the too-old-for-ten Randy. In the meantime Suzy was nodding her head, eyes growing bigger. As Randy elaborated on the fears and "scary chills" they had when their parents were fighting, he let us know that at least he knew what was going on since he was there to see it all. Going to school was too much to handle on Mondays because of the uncertainty factor. Neither child could be sure that when he or she came home the parents would also return. Better to stay home and be sick just to make sure Mom and Dad didn't pack up everything and disappear.

Apparently, the parents settled down during the week, perhaps because Dad became absorbed in his work, and the household was somewhat calmer. It was during the weekends, when leisure time confronted the couple, that the fighting would resume. So, we had an upset family, with parents unable to enjoy each other, Randy taking on the responsibility for his sister, and both children presenting physical symptoms of their emotional stress.

The parents entered counseling and gained insight into the causes of the children's unhappiness and psychosomatic symptoms. They stopped relating to them as "bad" children and took responsibility for their own immature behavior. This couple were so wrapped up in their fights, they forgot that they were parents. Several months of therapy stopped the weekend free-for-all, but the basic relationship had been so wounded that neither person felt any desire to stay together. The love was dead.

At least the divorce was not so stormy as the marriage. Dad did leave, but not at a gallop, nor with any hysterical crying on Mom's part. A follow-up of the children showed that their symptoms disappeared when the yelling stopped. Both are calmer now that their life style is defined. They know that Dad lives in an apartment and spends every other weekend with them. The weekends with Mom are no longer times of anxious worrying because their mother is happier and thus able to give them positive attention. The entire family also has learned how to talk about feelings instead of escaping by running away (Dad), taking to a tearful bed (Mom), or getting sick (the children).

This group of people had the advantage of psychotherapy. They are, however, in the minority of the population. Most divorcing couples have to manage on their own. If fortunate, during the crisis period they may have a friend or two who will give emotional support, minus any bad advice. More often than not, in our fast-paced society, splitting couples have no one to turn to for help. Parents may be in another state; city living does not foster neighborhood friendships; and, besides, it takes a very special and understanding friend to hold one's hand during the long, drawn-out procedure of divorce.

What happens to the millions of children who are also

suffering through a divorce? Distracted by their own feelings of guilt, failure, and remorse, most parents have little energy left to cope with children. When you become a stepparent, you may have to deal with children who never had the opportunity to express how they felt about the loss of a real parent through divorce. And it is a severe loss even though they may see the other parent regularly. What is lost is a sense of a whole family, even if it was a defective one, and even though in most ways everyone is better off now.

A forty-year-old man recently told us that at sixteen when his parents divorced he withdrew totally from his friends and activities. He couldn't bear to explain his family breakup to anyone. No matter, then, how old the children are, they must cope with their loss while continuing with the complicated process of growing up. Divorce is upsetting to everyone. However, our position is that, in the long run, it is better to divide a family, rather than remain together in misery. In other words, we have found that staying together "for the sake of the children" does them more harm than good.

The hundreds of children we have treated whose parents were divorced have a common idea—the persistent thought that they were at fault for the breakup. All children and adolescents normally think the world and its events revolve around them. They also think magically. That is, if they have a thought or a fantasy, they think they have actually performed that thought or fantasy. Since children think they have such powers, they automatically assume responsibility for their parents' breaking up. And they feel guilty. If they have been unable to talk about their feelings with an understanding adult, the guilt can become unbearable. Guilt-ridden youngsters will often begin behaving in antisocial ways such as lying and stealing. They usually get caught and are punished, thus relieving some of their original guilt. In later chapters we will discuss the art of helping children relieve their guilt by talking about feelings.

Children who have lost a parent because of abandonment or death suffer the same guilt or sense of responsibility. The surviving parent also must deal with this guilt when a mate dies or abandons the family. After all, the person did physically disappear, and the remaining members of the family are left to cope on their own. When faced with death, people experience a psychological reaction known as survivor's guilt. It is a feeling of "Why wasn't it me who died?" and "If only I had been there or done *something* different, that person would still be alive." This feeling gradually subsides as the shock of death wears off. The abandoned mate must cope not only with the same guilt, but also with the social embarrassment of explaining why one's partner just suddenly left, often never to be heard from again.

If you are a stepparent, you must understand what traumas your adopted family has experienced. If you are a single parent about to remarry, you should question yourself about how you coped with your experience of divorce or death. Have you really healed your wounds? Have you grown from the experience? Are the children stabilized? If you are a person who has left both mate and children, have you been able successfully to deal with the guilt that usually accompanies such a decision? How will this past action affect your relationships if you marry again and become a stepparent yourself? We promise you that it always does.

When couples experience divorce, whether desired or not, they always receive a blow to their self-esteem. A sense of failure is keenly felt for the wrong mate choice, the wasted years, and the inability to solve basic living and loving problems. In order to overcome this wound to self-esteem, a person must psychologically mourn the past marriage, just as one must mourn when a loved one dies.

MOURNING THE LOSS

We don't talk much about mourning in our society. No one can escape mourning, however, as death is the last event in our life cycle. Since no preparation is given, the feelings that arrive with loss can be overwhelming. Many people try to repress or bury these painful feelings and thus try to escape the natural mourning process. Unfortunately, such escapism does not work, and the person can become depressed, physically ill, or can even develop severe mental problems. This is especially true if the individual is prone to emotional conflicts.

Mourning must be experienced by adults and children alike. We must emphasize that even if you are the partner who sought divorce, and even if it was a good decision and you feel relieved to have it all ended, you will mourn nonetheless. For whatever happened in your marriage, you had invested yourself and your years.

Mourning has eight distinct phases:

DENIAL. You may have been present when a death or divorce was announced. The vast majority of people will exclaim, "Oh! No!" Children are more prone to continuing the denial phase of mourning, as they have no concept of death and little notion of time. A person who is left either by abandonment or by divorce can stay stuck in denial for a lengthy period, even for a lifetime.

Eunice, a woman in her early forties, was referred to us because of chronic fatigue, with no physical cause for her lethargy. Her husband, after twenty-two years of marriage, announced he was in love with another woman, left abruptly, and would deal with her only through his attorney. He immediately remarried and moved to another city. Her support checks were sent by an accountant. He made private arrangements to see their eighteen-year-old daughter. This break had occurred two years previously, but Eunice could not accept the reality of his cold approach to divorce, nor his sudden disappearance from her life. She felt as though he had made her an invisible woman.

Her ex-husband's cruel manner of handling the divorce gave Eunice no time to absorb the shock, no chance to find out why he stopped loving her and to compete for the return of his affection. After two years she was still in a state of emotional shock. Eventually, in therapy, she was able to understand that she was holding on to the fantasy that her ex-husband would some day come back to her, beg forgiveness, and they would resume their life together. She used so much energy daydreaming about this impossible magical solution, it is no wonder she was always tired. When she was able to accept reality, her appropriate anger could then be experienced. The unfelt anger toward her former mate also contributed to her fatigue. The next growth step was to begin to build her own life as a single woman.

Eunice's denial is not uncommon. Many rejected mates flounder in this first stage of mourning and waste their lives in longing for the past. They may even carry the corpse into the next marriage. This denial of reality has a negative effect on small children. They are eager to join in the denial and wait for the lost parent to return and make everything fine again. When they must finally accept the reality, it is far more difficult to manage than if they had been told the truth from the beginning.

GRIEF. The second phase of normal mourning is to give in to grief, that is, to allow all the tears to flow freely. It is a great mistake to exert control over one's wish to cry. We have heard parents say to children, particularly boys, "Now, you mustn't cry." Yes, we should all cry, sob, and moan if it serves to express and thus discharge the feeling of loss. Children should not be protected from a parent's sorrow. If they do not see genuine sadness over the lost parent, how can they feel safe in crying themselves?

PANIC. The third phase of mourning is a panic sensation that one must make sudden plans for the future. Unless there are immediate financial difficulties, the parent with the children should remain in the home. Everyone involved has enough to cope with already without being subjected to further sudden change. Moving, and adjusting to new schools, new faces, and a new environment are best done from a position of strength. If possible, stay where you are, thus simplifying responsibilities. Our advice to the parent who leaves the home is essentially the same. Make simple changes. Live close enough to your children so that you can assuage their fears that they will never see you again. Don't jump into another marriage immediately. You have to adjust also, even though you may have desired your freedom.

RIGHTEOUS QUESTIONING. If religious, mourning persons suddenly wonder why God is picking on them. Feelings of "why me?" or "life's not fair" begin to emerge. This rebellious questioning of the scheme of things is a preliminary symptom of the expression of underlying anger or rage.

ANGER. Getting in touch with the anger connected with loss is the fifth stage of mourning. Children have an easier time admitting their anger than adults. The reason is that children lack social reasoning, such as, "I should be gracious about being abandoned"; or, "It isn't nice to go around feeling furious." So kids can blurt out their anger while adults bottle it up. The trouble with repressing anger is that it surfaces elsewhere in a disguised form. It can take the shape of self-destructive activities. Newly divorced or bereaved people have more so-called accidents than the general population. These accidents can be minor ones (cutting oneself while cooking) or major ones (fatal falls or

auto wrecks). Repressed angry feelings can show themselves in physical illnesses like migraine headaches, ulcers,
or continual colds.

It is natural and normal to feel enraged. Acknowledge
your anger and seek an outlet for it. One of the soundest
ways to express anger is to have a nonjudgmental friend
listen to you as you vent your rage.

Recently a colleague of ours was going through a divorce after an eight-year marriage. He asked us out to
lunch. When he arrived at the restaurant, he looked pale
and said his doctor had just diagnosed a slight pneumonia.
He also said, "I've just got to bitch awhile," and proceeded
to complain, rant, and rave, and generally put down his
soon-to-be-ex-wife.

We listened but did not comment on his distortions
about the bad treatment he felt he had received. When he
finished, he brightened up and said, "All my congestion is
gone! I just had to get all that hate off my chest." He cured
his physical illness by discharging his anger. He also knew
that many of his feelings toward his former mate were
irrational, but that they needed to be vented in an atmosphere of acceptance.

If mourners do not deal with their anger, the repression
can affect future relationships for years to come. We suggest therapy during this time span if a person does not
have an understanding friend to lean on. Many women,
even in our enlightened era, feel that anger is unfeminine.
It is a mistake to assume that only men feel enraged and
have the right to express their feelings. Women must learn
to express their anger in healthy ways, such as actively
talking about it, rather than adopting the learned female
attitude of passive anger.

Jennifer, divorced six months, custodial parent of two
girls, became completely indecisive about minor details of
parenting. She would telephone her remarried spouse
several times a day, and always in the evening, usually just
as he was eating dinner. Because of his guilt over leaving

the children, he would patiently answer her childish questions. In the meantime his new wife was seething with resentment and jealousy over the time he was spending on the telephone. What Jennifer was really doing was invading their lives, appearing to be a helpless person. This passive approach to her anger (disguised as incompetency) only served to make two other people furious with her.

Jennifer's attorney, whom she also bothered with minute details, suggested therapy for her. Once the real feelings of rage were uncovered, Jennifer regained her former sense of competency. She learned that she was using her children to hide behind. She recognized her wish to invade her ex-husband's marriage and her secret enjoyment of the trouble she caused his new wife. When she could actively express her hateful feelings, she no longer needed to passively disrupt other people's lives. Once the anger was verbally discharged, Jennifer's psychological energies could flow into her own involvements.

MELANCHOLY. This form of depression tends to slow down a person's reactions to life. It is a necessary time of adjustment to a new life situation. If one has lost a mate through death, this melancholy helps to emotionally bury the dead. It's a quiet time when one turns inward, thinks over all the good and bad times together, deals with any lingering guilts over the finality of the loss. Many well-meaning friends and relatives make the mistake of trying to cheer up the melancholy mourner. What the person really needs is affection, a listening ear, and the knowledge that the mourner is still cared for by family and friends. This period may last anywhere from three months to a year. If it continues much beyond that, treatment should be sought to help the mourner move actively back into life.

GRADUAL RETURN TO NORMALCY. This stage involves a renewal of interest in other people, activities, work, and creative endeavors. Emerging from the melancholy of loss, the mourner becomes awakened to the ever-present needs of the children, the need for good health practices, and an overall sense of life's preciousness.

ACCEPTANCE OF THE LOSS AS A TOTAL LIFE EX-PERIENCE. If the loss was death, the mourner realizes that a part of his or her spirit will always carry some sadness for the departed one. Realizing that one can never replace that person is accepting reality. That one may love again is very likely, but each love will be different. This maturing experience makes people resolve to live life in a positive way, whether the loss was due to divorce or death.

When entering into new love relationships, persons who have mourned bring with them a more selfless approach to marriage. The trauma and stress of loss must be experienced, absorbed, and then used if one is to grow into a whole person. Any and all attempts to sidestep this profound human experience will affect future attempts to love and be loved.

Mary sought advice from us because of her husband's inability to forget his first wife. Mary had married Tom after he had been a widower for eight months. He had three children, aged three, five, and seven. They were all floundering. The children were cared for by a baby-sitter during the day, and Tom carried on in the evenings. He had so many responsibilities with his job and childcare that he felt the situation was hopeless. He was also grieving over his wife's sudden death in a plane crash. When he met Mary, her practical manner was a great help to him and his problems. She showed him how to simplify his approach to feeding and cleaning the children and getting them settled down for bed. She lightened his burdens through her love for him. The children were happier with a cheerful woman around, and it seemed natural that Tom and Mary would marry. The trouble was that although Tom loved his new wife, he felt guilty about loving again. He continually reminisced about his first marriage and often called Mary by his dead wife's name.

X
  After Tom came to see us, he learned that he was idealizing his first wife in order to avoid real intimacy with Mary. Since his original mate was human, she had had faults too. He was able to gain insight into his guilt and thus bury the past. The new family then began to grow closer as a unit and Mary no longer remained an outsider.

ONE-PARENT FAMILY

Statistics show that the majority of people remarry two or three years after the spouse's death or departure. What has occurred in the intervening years is quite significant to the adults and children in a one-parent family. All adults should have a grasp of how the years of living with one parent affect everyone concerned.

  For the divorced mother to end up with the children is still the norm. Although courts are giving more consideration to the father's request for custody, the mother still usually wins this court procedure. She is thrust into a new and difficult position. For even though the woman may spend the major part of her day taking care of children, the father's presence is felt, and he returns home to share the parenting chores. Mother now has the total day-to-day task of parenting. Emotionally distracted by the stresses of separation and divorce, she usually has little energy left to cope with children's demands.

  Financial reality forces the majority of divorced mothers to work outside the home. Also, the major share of discipline naturally falls to the mother. The visiting father becomes the playtime parent. He may feel guilty about leaving his children and thus spoil them during their days together. The situation has an unreal quality. The hassled mother may feel irritated, jealous of her former husband's freedom, and overwhelmed with her added responsibilities. The free parent may be suffering also, but, as any parent knows, it's easier to deal with personal problems without the presence of children.

Since children are quick to manipulate a situation, they may develop gimmicks to increase the visiting parent's guilt. Most children are angry about the family breakup anyway, and usually direct this hostility toward the mother.

One woman told us that her two daughters delighted in telling her about the beautiful restaurant where their Dad entertained them. Struggling to survive on a small income, the mother felt great resentment. The kids would elaborate about Dad's glamorous girl friend, who "just loves us so much." These girls were very bright and were consciously sticking the knife in with every tale of fun-with-Dad. Our advice was for Mom to put her foot down, directing the girls to stop the nonsense and instead talk about their angry feelings.

To her amazement, they were quite willing to say how mad they were. They both wondered why Mom couldn't keep Dad in love with her. They wanted him back home. They were afraid to tell their father about their dreams of his return because he might become angry and not see them again. All their descriptions of wonderful times with Dad were actually expressions of disguised angers and fears.

If the parents are reasonable about handling children's visits and discipline, everyone benefits. If you are the visiting parent, it is not fair to the children to allow them to manipulate your guilt, escape discipline, or receive too many expensive presents. It is also unhealthy for either parent to make the children decide whom they love more. Children usually love both parents. Sometimes they love one and not the other. In some instances, they hate them both. It is their right to have whatever feelings they actually have. One cannot invent feelings for another person nor can one legislate them.

The parent who tries to turn a child against the natural mother or father invariably loses the child's love and respect. If the other parent is really a horrible person, the child will discover that fact in time. Children have enough to deal with in accepting the divorce without being pulled into opposing camps. Neither should they be used to spy on the other parent. An exaggerated interest in the activities of the former mate is just an attempt to avoid the reality of loss.

The new role of the divorced mother isn't always overwhelming. She may be greatly relieved for having dissolved a painful relationship and feel happier as a result. Children respond well to a more contented mother. With every new accomplishment that the single parent achieves, her self-esteem grows. Learning to cope as a single parent adds to one's knowledge and self-confidence. One can also join a supportive single-parents group that meets to exchange ideas, organize trips, create baby-sitting pools, and often to provide new prospective mates.*

Many women we have talked with notice that divorce liberated them from some old-fashioned myths about themselves. One woman observed that she quickly learned to be an independent thinker. She had been programmed always to look to a man for decisions. She entered her second marriage as a confident person wanting to share life's responsibilities, rather than needing someone to take care of her.

Men who by choice or circumstance end up rearing the children develop a new attitude towards marriage. One man who spoke at a Parents Without Partners meeting declared that he had become a gentler person since caring for his four children during the last eight years. His wife had run away, leaving him with a brood of boys and girls ranging in age from one to seven. Before that, he had never changed a diaper, cooked a meal for five, or known the first thing about running a household.

*Contact your local Parents Without Partners for information and ideas.

He wisely took a three-week vacation just to sort things out physically and emotionally. His mother moved in temporarily and began to teach him the rudiments of childcare. She told him to forget about having a neat house and instead concentrate on the priorities. These were: four little ones who were abandoned, making plans for consistent help while he was at work, and taking each day at a time. Fortunately, he found a day helper, since he could not quit his job. In the evenings he was alone with his gang.

He stated that the biggest shock was the incredible sense of responsibility he felt for his children. He quickly learned the practical matters of housekeeping, but struggled with his worries and anxieties about his children's health, both physical and emotional. Finally, he learned to relax with them and also learned that the bond between him and his children was a beautiful thing that he would never have experienced if his wife had remained.

Bachelor fathers are increasingly popular in our society. The myth that we have absorbed from our cultural heritage, that only females can give mothering, is slowly fading. Men who choose to be the primary parent seem to enjoy their role and feel enriched by the experience. The children are likewise enriched.

Whatever the new family format may be, the stepparent enters a unique situation—namely, that the children have had the parent all to themselves for at least a year or two. Since all children enjoy this undivided attention, they have some rather strong reactions to a newcomer on the scene.

Chapter **2**

The Prospective Stepparent

THE CHILD'S POINT OF VIEW

Bill, ten, Ann, eight, and Tommy, six, all wait with great expectations for their father's once-a-month visit. He lives in Chicago. The children and their mother reside in New York. Dad arrives Friday after school to pick up the kids. Their first reaction is great joy as they climb all over him, eager to get going, filled with exaggerated expectations. However, when they leave the house for the ride to Dad's hotel, they all experience a sudden shock. Dad has another woman waiting in the car. They already know this lady, Sally, but wish she didn't come with Dad every time he visited. She's another person with whom they must share their father's attention. As all siblings do, they already are competing with each other. Who needs another competitor?

On the other hand, they want Sally to like them. At the same time, they resent her and feel jealous that Dad brings her along. Bill wants to talk about his football team, but feels restricted by Sally, who sits close to Dad. Ann wants to sit by Dad. Tommy wants to get some ice cream and begins to cry when no one hears his request. It was supposed to be a fun weekend. It has started out with hurt feelings on the part of all the children. Since children do not have the ability to hide their feelings very well, by the time the group arrives at the hotel suite, all the kids are cranky. Sally's attempts to brighten the conversation are met with silence. Dad feels upset and wonders what he has done wrong.

This scene is quite common in America today. You can see couples with children at the zoo on any sunny Sunday, enjoying a lot of misery. The man looks like the father of the youngsters, but the woman appears a little too young to have mothered the eleven-year-old. The atmosphere around these family groups is charged. The adults seem to be trying too hard to insure that the kids have a good time. The kids seem slightly obnoxious—more demanding, whiney, and clingy than normal for children on a recreational outing. Whenever children sense that adults are placating them, they feel uncomfortable and thus become more demanding. It also puts them one up on the manipulation scale. Trying to force a good time on children confuses them. Young people know they should not have so much power over an adult, so placating parents lose both the child's respect and their own authority.

Bill, Ann, and Tommy's father should have been more sensitive to their needs for his exclusive attention. If he were able to see them every week, a girl friend would not be such an adjustment for them. He placed an unnecessary emotional burden on all of them by insisting on bringing Sally with him. It would have been easier if they learned to relate to Sally during the summer weeks they spent in Chicago with Dad. This would also have the emotional advantage of being on familiar territory. It would have been simpler had he not even introduced his children to Sally unless the two of them had decided to marry. Many children are leery of having positive feelings toward their parent's dates because they may never see these strangers again.

ANTICIPATING READJUSTMENTS

To be realistic, a man's girl friend may not even like children. She too has a right to her feelings. She may resent sharing her well-earned weekends with a bunch of demanding kids. Children are quick to pick up negative feelings from adults and thus may feel rejected or, worse, that something is wrong with them. This sense of rejection begins a chain of events that leaves everyone climbing the walls.

Take, for example, Tammy and Lena, fourteen-year-old twin daughters of Fred. By mutual agreement, Fred has custody of the girls. The mother travels extensively, and thus her visits are sporadic. The girls feel more relaxed living with Fred because he's such an easygoing person. Their ambitious and energetic Mom is too nervous to handle adolescent problems.

Family life runs smoothly until Dad's occasional girl friend arrives for the weekend. The three females have a pleasant relationship. Cheri is a mother herself, so she assumes that young teenagers will be no threat to her. After Cheri is there for a while, she notices that Fred is too lenient with the girls and tells him so. In their typical teenage rags, the twins flop all over the house. They spend hours on the telephone, giggling with girl friends. They interrupt Cheri and Fred's conversations. By the end of the weekend, all pleasant feelings in the group have slowly deteriorated.

The girls feel confused, because their life style has been questioned by someone not even in the family. Cheri feels that she never gets any really private time with Fred, since the girls feel free to pop into the master bedroom in the morning to say "Hi!" The easygoing Fred feels pulled between the three females. He thinks the girls do their share of housework and cooking with no hassles. Their school grades are excellent and they have lots of friends. He also understands that teenagers are sloppy, giggly, and somewhat intrusive. Cheri's children have not reached this stage of development yet, so she interprets their behavior as a personal affront. These active teenagers really don't notice their bad habits, nor do they consciously want to interfere with their Dad and Cheri. Fred just wants life to run smoothly after all the ups and downs he experienced with his first wife.

What to do? If Cheri really values her time with Fred, she should read a couple of books about teenagers. Parents who have not reared adolescents do not understand this difficult stage of growth. It is a difficult time at best. A little knowledge is helpful when one must cope with people in the teen years. A lot of knowledge is even better. If Fred wants to continue to enjoy Cheri's company, he could make some visits to her house, taking a turn being the weekend stepparent for Cheri's children. Tammy and Lena are quite capable of taking care of themselves for a couple of days.

The weekend and holiday stepparent has to make several adjustments. If one is not already a parent, emotional and physical gears must shift. Instead of thinking only about one or two people, the weekend stepparent must consider three or seven people's needs. The weekend stepparent may also have to deal with resentment. The stepparent's time off is being spent on childcare duties, while the real mother or father is free to relax and enjoy the weekend.

This substitute parent may feel like he or she is being used by the children. By their nature young people are not especially grateful, and don't really care if someone spends three hours cooking an elaborate dinner for them. They probably prefer hamburgers and hot dogs anyway. Any fantasies that all weekends or holidays will run smoothly with children on the scene are unrealistic and self-defeating. We call it "thinking like a Norman Rockwell painting" —imagining life to be like his lovely picture of a Thanksgiving Dinner, with everyone sweet, pink, clean, and happy. Life just doesn't happen that way.

A friend of ours laughs now at her attempts to make the perfect Christmas dinner for her lover and his son and daughter, aged five and six. While she merrily cooked the goodies that went with her turkey, one of the little tykes turned the oven off. Since it was a self-basting turkey, our cook did not discover the deed until a half an hour before the feast. Their menu consisted of delicious hot dogs with cranberry sauce, sweet potatoes, brussel sprouts, and rolls. She has since learned to watch the oven dials. She has also discovered that kids may prefer hot dogs to turkey.

"You can't make it with children without a sense of humor," states one of our more mature friends. This credo is so true. For to take every act of children as serious or directed toward you personally will only age you prematurely.

Weekend stepparents may also be alarmed by the intensity of jealous feelings they feel toward the children. It is rather embarrassing to be jealous of a mere child. If you fall into the green pit, try to pull back a bit and rethink the situation. Remember that the child is probably in turn jealous of you because he has to share his parent with you.

You probably see your loved one during the week. The child most likely has strict visiting rules. The child's time with Mom or Dad is limited. So expand your own sharing capacities by understanding the child's needs. Remember that adults have more psychological resources than children. A jealous child can only cope with envious feelings by moping, crying, or shrieking "I hate you!" An adult ought to be able to cope with strong feelings, by injecting some reasoning. Empathizing with the child's feelings or verbalizing one's own also helps.

Bob fell in love with Lillian. They met at a large cocktail party and were immediately attracted to one another. When they began dating, Lillian always met Bob at a pre-arranged place. Their evenings were delightful to both of them. When they spent the night together it was always at Bob's apartment—just a cozy little love nest for two, free from the stresses and strains of outer reality.

His two boys were grown and gone from home, and thus the lovers' privacy was insured. Lillian explained that she never brought dates home with her as she felt it was unfair to her three daughters. "They know I have a love life, but they also know that it's private," explained Lillian. "I'll introduce you to them if we decide that we'll be together a long time."

This is practical thinking. In the search for a new life partner, one should expect to date many different people. Some relationships will be short, some long. Children do not need to see the experimental dates of their parents. Some resent the strangers. Some long for a new parent so desperately that they assume each new man or woman is the new father or mother. They can send a date scurrying away with remarks like, "Are you my Mom's husband yet?" or "When's the wedding? Can I come?"

When Bob finally met Lillian's three teenage girls, he really liked them. He said, "I was so much in love with that beautiful lady, I desperately wanted those girls to like me." His wish to be accepted by them caused Bob to rush in too fast. Teenagers are shy creatures. They like to size up an adult to make sure he or she is a "safe" person—"safe" meaning that the adult won't ridicule them or treat them as children.

Bob talked too much, gave too many compliments, and was generally anxious. The girls drifted away to their own activities, seemingly unimpressed. Poor Bob felt rejected and ineffectual. He confessed he didn't know very much about young women since he had only reared boys. Lillian's advice was to relax and to stop worrying about being accepted immediately. "They'll learn to like you, but gradually," was Lillian's advice. "Besides, they're more interested in who's going to call them and how they look than if they like you or not." True.

If you are a weekend stepparent, dating a person with children at home or children who visit, take it easy. The casual approach is the most successful one with children of any age. Be yourself. Kids can pick up phoniness faster than adults. Expect some resentment and jealousies from your lover's children. Rejection won't be such a surprise if you are armed with the expectation of its possible appearance. Just because the parent likes or loves you does not mean that his or her children will automatically think you're wonderful. Probably, just the opposite.

Remember that children make friends slowly with strange adults. Remember also that you are dealing with young people who have suffered through a divorce or a death in the family. Their past family life has been disrupted and disturbed. Because of the traumas they have lived through, these youngsters may be less mature and more sensitized than children from stable family situations. Make allowances for this immaturity and sensitivity, realizing that each child is unique and follows his own developmental pattern.

ACKNOWLEDGING PROBLEMS

Let us examine some of the negative aspects that a weekend stepparent may encounter. These real-life problems should be explored before a weekend stepparent decides to take the big step of becoming a permanent second parent.

The overly child-centered parent presents the most difficult situation for the dating partner to handle. This over-emphasis on "the kids come first" is usually a result of guilt on the parent's part. It is more prevalent in men than women, as the man is usually the visiting or visited parent.

If he has not resolved his guilt for "abandoning" his children, he may try to bribe them with expensive gifts or a complete lack of discipline.

Greed is a common quality of childhood. Guilty parents who try to "buy off" children will find themselves throwing gold into a bottomless pit. Children who sense that they can manipulate a guilty parent will demand an outrageous amount of material things. Since objects don't make anyone happy for very long, the guilty parent should recognize that bribes do nothing but increase the children's isolation from the parent, as well as enlarge their appetite.

One mother we knew felt so guilty about not providing a father for her son, she allowed him to interrupt her every conversation. This youngster was thoroughly despised by all her friends because he came first, no matter how important their adult discussion. Finally a tactful friend took this mother aside and explained that she was only doing her child a disservice. "He'll think he's so important that everything he has to say should be heard instantly. It'll be quite a shock to him when he starts school. He won't have the teacher's undivided attention," said her concerned friend. This unpleasant habit took some time for both mother and son to break, but she finally succeeded. The boy became a happier child once he lost his power to interrupt at will. Her devotion to his words was only a mask for her own guilt.

All children can be master manipulators if the parents allow this negative behavior. Although it may appear that the little ones enjoy manipulating, it doesn't make them feel very safe in the world. Adults are supposed to be in control of life.

A young nineteen-year-old man we treated stated that he would always resent his mother for allowing him to manipulate favors and expensive presents from her. He recognized that manipulating other people became a way of life for him. He never learned to earn his way because it was easier to con people. This attitude severely affected his relationships with teachers, friends, and girl friends. His mother had mistakenly assumed that she was gaining her child's love by giving in to all his desires.

Girls have an easy time manipulating guilty fathers, just as boys can easily con mothers. Ellen finally broke off with Matt because he always put his "Little Doll" Darla ahead of her. This nine-year-old girl was allowed total freedom of expression and was given anything she momentarily desired; and she would jump between Ellen and Matt whenever they sat down together. Matt also had an eight-year-old boy, who was expected to behave himself or was sent to his room. Even though Ellen pointed out the obvious favoritism toward Darla, he said he just couldn't resist his "Little Doll."

Ellen at first thought, "Well, it's only every other weekend and summers. I'll live with it." On clearer reasoning she could see that this child adoration would only get worse as time passed. She foresaw the boy's psychological suffering from the injustice of it all. Her love for Matt could not overcome her resentments and realistic fears. Matt was incredulous when he lost Ellen. He could not grasp the significance of his overidealization of his daughter. Now, years later, the girl has become a spoiled brat and expects to be the center of attention wherever she goes. Since the world at large relates to her as just another child, she always runs back to Dad for his unrealistic love. She will also run back to him when she finds herself in an unworkable marriage.

If you, as a prospective second parent, cannot get a guilty parent to recognize the damage that he or she is doing to the children, or if you cannot get the parent to seek counseling, consider a new relationship. For this behavior will not change once you marry. It may only increase. The fantasy that all will be changed after the wedding ceremony has broken up more second marriages than any other factor.

If you can talk over bad situations with your guilty

partner, then patience can be a rewarding trait. Child absorption comes from tortured feelings of loss. The guilty parent needs comfort, sympathy, and understanding during the initial mourning period. The objective adult can, without accusing, point out destructive patterns and be helpful in changing guilt into realistic parenting. To step aside and seethe about inadequate childcare is no act of friendship.

Parents are the most defensive people in the world when it comes to their interrelationship with their offspring. Tread lightly, but with care and concern, and you should be able to help a guilt-ridden parent toward insight. Your investment of patience and understanding will pay off in a deeper love and friendship with your partner.

Ellen realized that Matt was unable to balance her needs with his own and Darla's. This nonfulfilling relationship had no future. It is better to leave if the adult's needs come second to inappropriate demands of the children.

What tactics should you consider if you find yourself in love with a man or woman who is looking for a baby-sitter or disciplinarian? Some men still consider childcare strictly women's work. When the gang arrives Friday night, this man expects his weekend guest or daily companion to take over as "The Mom Person."

A careerwoman friend of ours with two daughters at home met this problem head on. She and Migel were in the same profession and had met each other at work. They were on an equal basis financially and had similar responsibilities. Migel had a girl and a boy, the same ages as Joan's two girls. As their romance deepened, the children all got to know each other and played well enough together. Migel suggested an engagement period during which they would all live together for the summer. Since Joan had a house big enough to accommodate all of them, Migel and children moved in.

Suddenly, Joan discovered that Migel's night meetings tripled and that she was often left with four youngsters to feed, bathe, and bed down. Migel wanted her to sell her small sports car and buy a van for the family. He, of course, would keep his flashy import. Other clues were popping up, such as Migel's laissez-faire attitude concerning discipline. If a loud squabble began between the four youngsters, he feigned deafness and Joan was obliged to referee.

Joan turned the tables. One night when Migel arrived home, Joan was on her way out the door. As he stood in the living room disbelievingly, Joan said she was having dinner with friends and would probably go to the theater after dinner. "But what about dinner for the kids?" the unwilling Dad asked. She breezed off. When she returned late that night to her angry partner, she pointed out his obvious wish to place her in the total-parent role. Being demoted from peer to second-class baby-sitter was not Joan's idea of a new living situation. Since Migel really was looking only for a new mother for his offspring, he soon departed. Joan was relieved to have learned of his plan before she and Migel had made any permanent commitment.

We've all seen women with unruly children who pretend they are helpless to control the little beasts. They arrive at your house and promptly expect the first available male to take over the discipline. This you-do-it attitude was espoused by Lucille, who thought of herself as too frail a woman to handle her two boisterous boys. They loved to wrestle anywhere and at any time, with accompanying whoops and hollers. Whenever she became involved with a man, she expected him to subdue her monsters. Since most men do not care to be used in this fashion, Lucille is still looking for Mr. Superman and the boys are still banging around.

If you are involved as a weekend stepparent with a person who still thinks that only women should run the vacuum or that only men should control the children, you are walking into a constricting way of life. If you share the same role expectations, then you will be comfortable. If you do not, remember that love does not conquer all, particularly sexist attitudes. There are enough personal adjustments to make in a new marriage without having to battle role-playing too.

RECOGNIZING PSYCHOLOGICAL MISFITS

Another characteristic to look out for as a future stepparent is parental indifference or cruelty in your partner; that is, watch out for the person who physically or psychologically abuses his or her own children. The man who announces he can't stand kids, but who must care for them once a month, betrays himself as a basically unfeeling man. He may be gentle and kind with his lover and yet show no affection toward his children. Whether they remind him of the disaster of his past marriage or not is no excuse for mental abuse. He helped to bring the children into the world and they deserve more than cold treatment. That same uncaring attitude can easily be transferred to a new wife. Besides, it is difficult for a nonparent to stand by and watch innocent children suffer because of their real parent's indifference.

If you consider yourself a responsible person, point out these cold qualities to your partner. But do it in private, please; and with gentleness, for indifferent parents may be unaware of how they are hurting their child. They may very well be repeating a pattern from their own childhood. Nonetheless, if a child does not feel any love coming from a parent, that child feels unlovable and worthless. This psychological atmosphere is not a good growing environment for the child's self-esteem. If you are willing to help the abusive parent, you can also give some loving attention to the ignored child. Whatever appropriate positive attention a child receives will help him or her face the challenges of life.

Ignoring abusive behavior will work only if you see the parent and children together infrequently. Marrying an uncaring parent will only mean that you will be taking on an incredibly difficult and thankless task.

One of the most common complaints that we hear from children of divorced parents is that the children were forced to take on adult responsibilities that they could not handle. In such cases, the parents actually make their own children assume parental roles. The children feel responsible for the adult's grief and assume the task of nursing the regressed parent. Whether the children express it or not, they are plenty angry about this unfair reversal of roles; for it robs them of their childhood and adds worries to their already upset lives. We call such children "pseudo-adults."

The weekend stepparent may end up receiving the hostility that this pseudoadult has bottled within. Since the regressed parent cannot deal with normal anger, a stranger can easily become the target for the rage. Also, if the child has become accustomed to the parental role, the youngster may be jealous of an intruder taking over. Many parents make the grave mistake of telling their child, "You are the man/woman of the house now that Dad/Mom has gone." They are not. They remain children, with one parent.

Psychological immaturity in the prospective mate may not reveal itself at once. Sara was swept off her feet by seductive Charley. He was so persuasive, charming, and sexually exciting that in a matter of months Sara left her husband of one year and married Charley. Just that fast, without ever meeting his children! They seemed so remote, way off in another state. When it came time for his two daughters' summer visit, Sara was thrown into a state of confusion and rage. For not only was Charley seductive with Sara, but also blatantly so with his fourteen- and fifteen-year-old girls. He flirted, teased, made eyes and suggestive remarks to them. They loved it and gave Sara contemptuous looks when she appeared disapproving.

One day when Charley and his "little sweethearts" were out by the pool, wife number one telephoned. She needed to make plane reservations for the girls' return trip. She asked Sara, "Is Charley still flirting with the girls?" Sara said, "Definitely!" and asked what in the world she should do about this destructive behavior. Wife number one replied, "Beats me. That's why I divorced the jerk!" Not very helpful advice, but realistic. It turned out that Charley was that way with all ladies.

Men who must continually prove themselves by conquest of each new woman they meet do not make good mates. This Don Juan syndrome originates from poor male self-esteem. But men like Charley rarely seek a remedy, as they think they're having such a good time. They usually end up alone and lonely, for only a masochistic female will put up with being humiliated by a Charley's wanderings. Sara left, and sought treatment to discover why she picked out such a louse.

Boys who have been pushed into the "little man" role are usually quite angry little boys. A part of the task of being a child is to grow independent of the mother. If she keeps him tied to her for company, acts seductively with him, or relates to him like a pseudoadult, he is caught in the miniature-husband bind. These boys usually speak sarcastically to their mothers when they are in public. They demand and get any trip or favor they want. Mom is usually afraid to say no, because she will then lose her miniature man.

These unhealthy dependent mother-son or father-daughter relationships are difficult for any prospective stepparent to handle; for this pact of dependency is usually buried deep in the unconscious of the parent and the child. Even though the adult may yearn for a new mate, he or she already has a small wife or husband in the house.

The clearest indication of this strange bond is if the visiting stepparent is not allowed to discipline the misbehaving minispouse. This kind of child will test the intruding adult as soon as he or she senses the parent's interest in a new mate. Unfortunately, these children often succeed in driving away prospective new fathers or mothers, and with the unspoken consent of the parent. However, eventually these minispouses grow up and leave home, but they tend not to have emotionally rewarding lives. The abandoned parent becomes depressed and either withdraws from society or seeks psychotherapy.

THE RIGHT TO EMPLOY DISCIPLINE

The weekend stepparent must meet the problem of discipline very early in the relationship. Never allow yourself to be a doormat. If children sense that you feel you have no right to correct their bad behavior, manners, or habits, they will gleefully continue to be progressively obnoxious. Children need limits. They don't always like them, but controls and frustrations are necessary ingredients for growing up. If a prospective mate will not allow you to discipline when you are a weekend stepparent, the pattern will only accelerate if you marry.

The discussion of limits and controls should take place away from children's ears. If they hear your discussions, they can manipulate you by arguing, "Mom says I don't have to do what you say." If you are going to share another person's life and children, then the two of you must present a united front. Disagreements can and should be thrashed out in private. If you pretend indifference to limits, but inwardly seethe, you are being dishonest to yourself and all concerned. All parties involved will suffer for your dishonesty.

A good point was made at a recent stepparenting seminar we conducted. A biological mother turned to a woman contemplating stepparenting. The soon-to-be-married lady was feeling guilty about her wish that the kids would grow up and get out. The real mother said, "What makes you think that biological parents don't hate their kids half the time?" The never-before-married woman was vastly relieved. Another myth of parenting exposed.

Before you make a decision to take on an instant family, dwell on the points we have explored. If you feel you have the extra love and understanding it takes to rear someone else's children, then our best wishes go with you. If you don't have the emotional stamina, better to admit it, accept it, and look for the rare specimen who is childless. Be honest with yourself. You will be no less of a person for it, just a more realistic one.

Chapter 3

Building a Strong Marriage

BUILDING A SOUND LOVE RELATIONSHIP

In our society swift decisions and actions are admired cultural traits. Speed may be an essential element of success in business, but it is not so in relationships. It is easy to fall in love, but difficult to sustain romantic feelings. Though millions of people marry and subsequently divorce, they enter new marriages with blind optimism. Unfortunately, they still carry with them the same magical notions about marriage as when they took their original marriage vows; that is, "Everything is going to be beautiful between us. We are in love, so why worry."

Love is one of the most powerful forces in human nature. Without love, a human being is a pitiful creature, for his or her life is meaningless and without substance. But love is also frail, needing the daily nourishment of support and affection.

In our society, love between man and woman has many barriers to overcome. From the time children enter school

35

until adolescence, they are encouraged to compete in the boys-against-girls game. Children may also absorb this division of the sexes in their homes. Favorite cliches— "woman's work," "a man's job," "crazy female drivers," and "men don't cry"—all have an impact on the impressionable child.

When the normal childhood sexual drives are rekindled at puberty, boys and girls begin to relate romantically to each other. Sadly, however, they have lost something in the seven- or eight-year interim. The contrived barriers between the sexes interfere with an understanding of the opposite sex. It is okay to fall in love as a teenager, but it is not okay to relate as friends before that time. So young people fall in love, but they do not become friends. This attitude carries through into marriage.

Consider this: if you have a violent disagreement with a friend, you can argue, shout, and resolve the issue because you have the friendship to bind you. If lovers have an argument, there is a sense of panic that all is lost, because the frail love bond does not have a foundation in friendship. Lovers tend to idealize each other. When a personality fault is exposed between lovers, the disappointment is great. This is not the case between friends.

Friendship takes a long time to grow and deepen. Love can happen in a matter of minutes. A friend is a person you can trust. Trust means that a friend sees and accepts your strengths and weaknesses. A friend can be trusted to not hurt your feelings intentionally. A friend is emotionally supportive when you are feeling down. A friend shares your happiness and dreams with you and is quick to celebrate your successes. A friend is affectionate and warm. A friend is also dependable when you need a favor, advice, or companionship. A friend tries to be nonjudgmental, but nonetheless won't let you make a fool of yourself.

You can be yourself with a friend because you feel totally accepted. You can confide in a friend, knowing that your privacy will be respected. A friend can play with you, enjoying your carefreeness and ability to act silly. You can tease a friend without fear that he or she will misunderstand your comments as being hostile.

The ease and psychological freedom you experience with a friend take time, mutual life events, and open conversations about yourselves. A deep and meaningful friendship increases one's self-esteem because of the effort and care extended toward another person. Most people have friends of the same sex, largely because of the unnatural barriers set up between boys and girls during childhood.

Lovers relate to each other on a more physical or sexual level. Lovers show their "good" sides to each other. Lovers try to repress differences rather than work them out. Lovers spend a lot of time in bed, which is a delightful recreation. Making love well is much easier than making friendship. If anyone lacks love-making expertise, there are many books written to help the novice. Making friends is not so easy to do because it takes so much time and effort, so much giving and vulnerability.

ROMANCE IS NOT ENOUGH

The point is that people who fall in love should strive to make friendship a foundation for their love—particularly, parents who remarry. Because of the additional problems they are going to encounter, prospective stepparents should begin the marriage as friends as well as lovers. There should be no need to rush into marriage just because two people fall in love.

Ken said he met Marilyn over the yogurt section of a health-food store. Their common interest in nutrition led to a date that night. Within a month, they were married. Ken, a spiritual person, was accustomed to living in a frugal manner. Marilyn had two children. She was previously married to a very wealthy man. The children had been used to servants and could barely tie their own shoes.

Ken said it took him a year just to teach the children to do minimal chores, such as cleaning their rooms or taking out the garbage.

The boy and girl would spend three summer months with their father and return home spoiled rich kids. The father was always sending his children expensive presents and judged other people by their material worth. He spoke about Ken as though he were a failure as a man because he didn't earn a lot of money. The children picked up the same attitude and made life unpleasant. Unknown to Ken, because they were virtual strangers when they married, Marilyn was also a materialist. The marriage, based on sexual attraction, did not last.

A solid marital relationship is woven with the threads of sexual love and friendship. Anyone who has been married before is deeply aware that problems cannot be solved by jumping into bed, or wherever. You can solve problems by talking openly, which is easy to do if you're friends. You can tell a friend that his or her children are acting out of line. Tell that to a lover, and your beloved will automatically feel personally threatened and rejected, and will withdraw love.

Just because you may have been programed to believe that people of the opposite sex are a mystery does not mean you cannot learn about the other sex. We all share the need to be loved, accepted, and cared for by others. That's a good starting point. Get to know your prospective life partner, as a person as well as a lover. You will enrich both your life and your marriage, and will have more emotional energy for the children whom you will parent.

The children in your families will learn to know their second parents before the wedding, if you allow yourselves time to develop a friendship. The shock of another adult in their lives will be reduced if the children have had the opportunity to learn to like and trust their new parent. A major fringe benefit of such an approach is that, by watching you and your partner develop a friendship, the children will learn that they too should become friends with the other sex when they grow up.

As a prospective stepparent you may discover, during an extended courtship, that you do not like your lover's children at all. They may not like you either. There are some people combinations that are unworkable. You should give yourself sufficient time to weigh the possibility of whether the mutual dislike will affect the marriage. After six months, you can make a wiser decision than you would have made had you brushed your negative feelings aside with the "love can handle all" myth.

A childless couple have a great advantage over parents ✗ who marry. That is, they have the privacy to adjust to each other and work out living patterns, and the opportunity to enjoy each other's exclusive attention. If they eventually create a child, the new parents have already established a critical bond between themselves. This luxury is not available to a stepparent, for he enters into a group already formed. Children's needs must be met and cannot be shelved while parents make the necessary adjustments with each other. This is another argument in favor of a long courtship before entering a stepparent situation.

KEEPING YOUR LOVE ALIVE

The number-one priority in your lives should be your marriage. The love and, hopefully, the friendship that brought you two together should grow richer with the years. The partner who was married before will most likely be the more mellow of the two, for experiencing marriage, childbirth, divorce, or death is a maturing process. Remarried people tend to be more understanding, accepting, and more motivated to succeed the second or third time around.

It isn't easy to maintain romantic feelings, but it is possible. Romance involves an absorption with one's lover. His or her emotional needs are considered top priority and are gladly met without a feeling of sacrifice. Sexual love does not mean just sexual intercourse. It is also the little pats, hugs, and kisses when couples are together. It is cuddling in bed during the night. It is cooking especially loved dishes for each other. It is giving sincere attention in conversation. It is mothering each other when sick.

Virginia and Bill married after several years of single parenting. Their marriage combined five children, all teenagers. As we have discussed, the adolescent years are filled with turmoil. This family of seven was, after a year of marriage, ready for breakup. The adults were confused by and disappointed with the deterioration of their love for each other. Their jobs were demanding, the children took up the majority of their home time, and they never seemed to have any energy left for each other. Virginia and Bill entered counseling as a last resort before divorce. They discovered that from years of being single parents, they both paid too much attention to their teenagers. Actually, all the youngsters could have been self-reliant, but had grown used to depending on their parents for rides, advice, and daily care.

At the therapist's suggestion, Virginia and Bill took a long-overdue honeymoon. The lack of responsibilities on the vacation gave this couple a chance to sort out their difficulties. They realized that they were spending too much physical and emotional energy on their children, simply out of habit. They also recognized that they should simplify their overextended social life and spend their valuable free time with each other.

The children soon responded to the change in their all-attentive parents and learned to be independent. By concentrating on each other's need for love and affection, Virginia's and Bill's romantic feelings soon returned. Now, after work, they make sure they have their special time for each other. They made a small sitting room in their bedroom. They retire there for an hour and, although it may sound simple, they refresh their love every day. The children take turns preparing dinner while the adults sit, hold hands, and have a cocktail. They plan to continue their love ritual even when the children leave home. They both say that this special time rejuvenates their spirits after a demanding day. They also have taught their children to respect their privacy and their need for love.

Childcare duties do not have to interfere with or interrupt romantic love. All children can learn that parents need their privacy. You don't have to have dinner with the children all the time. If you lead a particularly stressful life, you may not wish to eat with them at all. This is especially true if dinner is the only private time available for you and your partner. It is healthy to be selfish in this respect.

Many adults forget that everyone needs a daily supply of affection. Human beings, male or female, are not being weak when they feel the need to be told they are loved, when they want to be kissed and hugged, or when they desire sexual attention. It is a sign of maturity to admit the need to love and be loved.

A big factor in growing intimacy is giving little gestures of affection to one another. To let a day pass without many expressions of love is a wasted day. Love is being aware of your partner's needs and then meeting those needs. The little gestures can include bringing your mate coffee in bed, patting each other while sitting together, asking how the person is feeling, doing errands for each other, giving a foot rub or massage, saying "I love you" and why, caring about office complaints, drawing a bath, teasing good-naturedly, giving compliments, holding hands when walking together, writing love letters, or hugging and kissing when leaving or coming home. When your children and stepchildren grow up in an atmosphere of creative thoughtfulness, they will assume that this behavior is natural and will act this way toward their future mates.

All of these acts of love add to the joy of sexual expression between two people. They can be considered as emotional foreplay, and they do enhance actual intercourse. To be a creatively loving partner also makes life intensely enjoyable, as it adds to your self-esteem. And the delight in doing helpful things for each other will be felt by the children in your home. Seeing your loving attitude will give them a positive mental image of what a marriage should be. As they leave home to make their own lives, they will seek to copy your life-style.

Part **II**

NORMAL CHILD
DEVELOPMENT
AND PARENTING

Besides the special problems that stepparents and prospective stepparents face in rearing their stepchildren, they also will have to deal with the usual questions and frustrations that all parents encounter in guiding the psychological development of their children. All humans journey through complex psychological stages from infancy to death. Knowledge of these life stages will help the novice parent or stepparent understand and help children as they wend their way toward adulthood. Although the chapters in Part II only briefly touch the surface of psychosexual development, they do provide valuable background for understanding this vital human theory.*

When evaluating yourself as a parent or stepparent, please remember that no one handles this responsibility perfectly. Understanding the growing child's psychological stages will facilitate the job; but the soundest approach to good parenting is using your own common sense. This, mixed with love, discipline, and the setting of appropriate examples, will do the best job.

*Please see the list of Suggested Reading on pages 143-145 for additional information in this area, particularly Theodore Lidz.

Chapter 4

Infancy and the
Toddler Years

FIRST INFLUENCES

A baby's development begins at conception. The developing organism has responses to the fetal environment, as seen in birth defects caused by viral infection of the fetus. The fetus can also be affected by the mother's psychological condition. More and more studies show that upset pregnant women produce hyperactive infants. That is, many of the chemical changes that the woman undergoes as a result of negative emotional reactions pass through the placenta into the infant. Thus, an infant's first experiences in life, even while still in the womb, can have an effect on the baby's future personality. During and after birth, many influences may affect the newborn: a mother's fears may prolong labor; the immediate handling of the newborn can be gentle or unfeeling; the infant may be taken from the mother immediately after birth for many hours. Many obstetricians are learning the value of "rooming," a system where mother and child occupy the same room while hospitalized. This arrangement facilitates the development of the bonding feelings so important for both mother and infant.

THE INFANT YEARS

The first stage of psychosexual development, after birth, is called the *oral period*. As this label suggests, the infant's needs center exclusively around the mouth. Babies are born with an instinctive drive to suck; and, of course, in order for the infant to survive that drive must be satisfied through feeding.

However, this stage of life involves more than the child's need for nourishment. A baby also requires love, warmth, a sense of safety, and physical stimulation. It is in this first stage of life that the helpless infant learns whether to trust the world or to experience life negatively. Babies learn to feel trust if their needs are met in a loving fashion by a nurturing adult.

Breast-feeding, if the mother enjoys the closeness of nursing, is the best insurance for a child's sense of being loved. The contact with the mother's skin; the sound of her heartbeat (which the baby heard in the womb); the position of the infant's head, which encourages mutual eye contact—all feed positively into the baby's growing sense of self. Breast-feeding also continues and intensifies the bonding experience between mother and child. Nature's way is the most healthy way. Tampering with nature's way is usually dangerous.

Mother's milk contains antibodies that help protect the baby from various early infectious diseases. Practically speaking, the nursing mother has many advantages over the woman who bottle-feeds her infant. No need to prepare the formula because baby's food goes along with Mom. The nursing mother's uterus regains normal size more quickly, because sucking promotes uterine contractions. Sucking also generates genital sensations in the mother. This erotic component is another bonding facilitator and adds to the pleasure of nursing. Some women feel embarrassed or guilty when they experience sexual enjoyment while nursing. There is no need to feel guilty about a completely natural and human experience.

The nursing mother thus colors the child's first relationship in life with a very positive tone. The child relates to the breast and to a living person. A bottle-fed baby relates to a thing rather than a person.

Although we are strongly in favor of breast-feeding, we understand that some women just do not feel comfortable with the idea of nursing. Of greatest significance is the nature of the total situation between mother and infant. An unwilling nursing mother who feels she "must do the right thing" will transmit her anger or anxiety to the sensitive infant, who will then become fretful. Mothers should choose whichever method gives them the most serenity. The important beginning stage of life can then be as mutually satisfying as possible. Bottle-fed babies should be held at every feeding just as nursing babies are.

The psychological bond between mother and child is first established during pregnancy and birth. Then the bond is strengthened by the nurturing mother. The manner in which she tends to the infant's requirements—nursing, changing diapers and clothes, bathing, rocking and playing—will be stored in the baby's emotional memory bank as "this is what life is all about."

By the term *emotional memory bank* or *unconscious* we mean the psychological driving force within the human psyche which is totally unknown to the individual but which is present from birth on (and probably before). Its components are made up of *all* life experiences since birth (and maybe since conception).

You can visualize the emotional memory bank better if you think of it as an emotional tape recorder. Whatever is imprinted on the person's tape is perceived as normal for that person. For example, a child is born to a depressed mother. Her mothering will be tinged with gloom; she will be unable to relate joyfully to her infant's needs; certainly her face and sweat will communicate negative states. This kind of mothering makes an infant anxious and fretful. It will also be recorded on the baby's emotional memory tape that potentially good things in life can bring on anxiety and a sense of doom and gloom.

On the other hand, if a child is born to a happy and contented woman who delights in her child's needs, that infant's emotional memory bank will contain the imprint that life equals being loved. No one can remember all one's life experiences. We all have partial childhood and adolescent amnesia. However, one part of our brain has stored within it all past experiences.

Other influences are also at work on a beginning person during early infancy. A baby is not born a blank canvas, for each person has inborn instinctual drives for survival. The instincts are fueled by human sexuality and aggression. The latter makes the infant cry and scream, whereas the former causes hunger. The infant is totally concerned with itself only and has no ability to empathize with another person's needs. These instinctual drives remain little changed throughout life. They do become greatly modified, however, in the process of a person's learning social manners.

All babies are also born with predetermined genetic capacities that will affect their psychological and physical growth. These inherited givens are intelligence, creative gifts, and many body characteristics. The baby's sex and appearance also affect the parents' response to the child. There is no point in denying such subjective responses. The mother who longs for a girl and delivers a boy is going to transmit her disappointment to the infant. Her somewhat rejecting attitude will be recorded on the child's emotional memory tape.

During the first stage of life the infant also begins to develop abilities to cope with life. The baby is born with one familiar coping device, namely, crying. Some people never develop coping mechanisms other than crying.

During this first phase of development, the infant's sense of self begins to grow. Remember that this sense of self is fed primarily by the nurturing mother. The child's sense of self also is affected by secondary bonding relationships such as with the father, siblings, grandparents, or whomever. The sense of self can be inferior if the child is unwanted or unloved, just as the wanted and cherished infant will perceive him- or herself as an "okay" person. This sense of self grows along with the child throughout the developmental stages and becomes solidified in adulthood.

Your stepchildren's developmental stages were most likely incomplete in one way or another. Their parents had obvious irreconcilable differences which must have had an impact on their parenting. The stepparent who is a loving and concerned person has an opportunity to correct the stepchildren's view of themselves if they did not receive the love due them as infants. The stepparent has a chance to lay a new track on the emotional tape recording. This corrective mothering or fathering may take some years to bear fruit, but the rewards of an emotionally healthy child are great indeed.

Babies in the infancy stage (from birth to approximately fifteen months) should be developing coping devices other than just crying. They learn that babbling and cooing bring forth delight and smiles from the mother. They also develop skills such as drinking from a cup, feeding themselves finger foods, talking, crawling, and walking. It's an exciting time to be watching infants, as they grow and learn the delights of exploring the world, first visually, then experientially.

Infants who do not receive adequate nurturing during the oral stage of life can become fixated at this level of growth. Obesity, alcoholism, and compulsive talking are signs of infantile neglect at the first stage of life. Although we all retain sensual residues of the oral period (smoking, kissing, talking, drinking, eating, and chewing gum), the deprived infant becomes the miserable adult still seeking pleasure through his mouth.

The mouth is the most sensualized organ, giving the baby tremendous pleasure, but the infant also experiences genital sexual feelings. Many boy babies are born with erections from the stimulation of the birth canal. Girl babies experience genital pleasure when they are first bathed and the washcloth makes genital contact.

The greater the amount of loving attention the infant receives during the dependent and helpless oral stage, the more quickly the child will move to the next task of growth.

Many children carry transitional objects from one phase to another. These objects are replacements for the nurturing mother. Relating to people and things other than mother is a sign of healthy personal resources in a child. The most common transitional object is the child's baby blanket, or parts thereof. Older infants suck their thumbs (a replacement of the soft breast). Using this personal resource is an example of beginning independence from the mother. The baby is learning self-gratification, rather than being totally dependent on the mother for pleasurable sensations.

These abilities are the first roots of *sublimation*, which is the ability to direct drives into channels other than the original objects of the drives. The baby redirects the need to suck the nipple to sucking the thumb or to rubbing a blanket. We will also see the growth of the ability to sublimate in future developmental stages.

Sometime between ten and fifteen months, taking into consideration the tremendous variations in rate of human development, a child should start to be weaned from the breast or bottle. The more sucking satisfaction the child has received during early infancy, the easier it is to accept weaning. Babies who have been given a cup from which to drink (starting at six to ten months) may very well wean themselves. Sometimes self-weaning causes a feeling of rejection in the nursing mother, since the baby will no longer totally depend on her for nourishment.

The weaning process should be done gradually to allow infants to accommodate themselves to self-gratification. Some increase in thumb- or finger-sucking may be noted during weaning. Sucking is the child's immediate comfort resource, and the baby should not be restricted from this pleasure.

Between twelve and fifteen months infants will usually develop another coping tool. They will begin to learn the rudiments of language. The more they are spoken to, the more quickly older infants will respond by imitating their parents' voices. Their ability for socializing increases with language.

All new skills—grasping and holding objects, babbling and talking, crawling and walking—add to the infant's growing sense of self. If the mothering person who cares for the child's needs is appropriately pleased with the baby's new skills, this positive attention gives the infant a boost in self-confidence and self-love. An attentive parent also imprints on the infant's growing memory tape that loving attention can be gained by learning new skills.

Loved infants, by fifteen months, are a delight to observe. They glow with curiosity, constantly explore their small world, give and receive affection, and are sensitive to their parents' likes and dislikes. Healthier kids already show the rudiments of a sense of humor. Unloved infants, by comparison, are usually retarded in development, both physically and emotionally. They are dull and unresponsive, and they generally suffer from more upper-respiratory diseases than the average child. This runny-nose syndrome is a sublimated form of crying and can be a symptom that announces the child's unhappiness.

Love is food for an infant's growth. If they do not receive loving care, some babies can even die. This disease, so common in orphanages of the past, is called *marasmus*— a wasting away from self-enforced starvation.

Maternal deprivation has a lifetime effect on a person's ability to love and to relate to others. Abandoned babies will grow up to be anxiety-ridden adults. Their emotional tape has recorded that life equals abandonment. Battered children will very often become battering and abusive parents.

THE TODDLER YEARS

Around fifteen months the child enters a new stage of development. The mother must take on a new role at this time. Previously, the nurturing mother met the infant's needs for food, love, and socializing. She must now teach the child how to become a member of the household with its specific rules of behavior. She is also guardian against the dangers present in a home for a curious toddler.

At this stage, children will begin to learn that they must now earn love and approval by conscious self-control. In earlier infancy they received unqualified love. Now, in the toddler stage, they must develop emotional skills to earn and deserve love. They will also begin to learn about ambivalent feelings toward the mothering person—feelings of both love and hate toward a person at the same time. The all-giving mother now becomes the demanding and frustrating mother.

Toddlers are still mostly all instinctual drives. The self-centered instincts send the message, "Pretty flowers. I want them. Grab." If the child's sense of self has grown properly, the toddler will have some concern about grabbing anything in sight, for mother disapproves of indiscriminate grabbing and she may withdraw her love and approval. The toddler may be able to exercise control in a limited way.

The toddler will have heard the first "No!" soon after beginning to ambulate around the house. This is the beginning of the development of the child's conscience. The conscience is the inward sense of justice, the sense of right and wrong. These absorbed parental notions of right and wrong do not become fully solidified until late adolescence. If the parent issues too many declarations of "no" or "bad, bad baby," the child's conscience or inner judge can become too harsh. The child will become a limited person, fearful of initiative and lacking in self-confidence. The parent who lacks maturity and gives the toddler too few "no's" will rear a spoiled child, lacking respect for others' possessions and privacy.

This stage of psychosexual development is termed the *anal stage*, and lasts to approximately three years of age. During this period the child's source of sensuality switches from the mouth to the anal region. It is the time of bladder and bowel training.

The anal period, however, involves a great deal more than just learning how to control the bladder and bowels. As toddlers enter more deeply into family life, they develop a sense of initiative, but their parents begin expressing their need for the child to conform to family rules. The child's growing self-concept becomes obsessed with a sense of independence. Ask any two-year-old if he or she would like to have lunch, go for a walk, or say "hello" or "goodby," and the automatic response will be a resounding "No," even if the toddler wants to eat, walk, or talk. This negative attitude is a symptom of young independence and should not be cause for alarm.

Many demands are placed on little children during the toddler years. They must feed themselves, learn language, test parental demands of behavior, attempt bowel and bladder control (with the connected erotic feelings), cope with older or new siblings, and attempt to earn love and attention, as well as explore their world.

It's no wonder that toddlers and young walkers are often irritated, and prone to temper outbursts. They have a small sense of themselves that is having a difficult time coping with many frustrations. When the demands of this complicated growth period become excessive, toddlers will regress to the infancy stage and suck their thumbs. For burdened two-year-olds, it's like finding a haven in a storm. After some brief self-gratification, they will forge forth to new adventures.

Consistent parenting is extremely important during this stage. Toddlers have so many behavioral rules to learn that they do not need their lives muddied by mixed messages. They receive mixed messages, for example, when the parents allow them to play with the TV knobs one day, but are furious the next time they attempt to fiddle with the set. Toddlers' curiosity and obstinacy push them to test parental rules over and over again. If they should not stick a finger in this light socket, how about the one across the room? If they cannot hit baby brother with one hand, how about the other?

Sublimation is learned during the toddler period with a subsequent increase in coping skills. It is not all right to smear feces all over the wall. This wish can be sublimated by playing with mud or by finger painting on paper.

Toddlers use their new language to gain attention. They replace crying with talking and asking. If bowel control occurs during this time (sometimes it doesn't), children feel a great sense of accomplishment; and proud parents who are generous with praise add to their growing self-esteem.

Toddlers' days are filled with mastery and disappointment. Mature parents give the children room to grow and learn. Overprotective parents, fearing that the children cannot handle the frustration of failure, will stunt their development, since frustration pushes children toward maturity and toward becoming persons richer in experience.

Although two-year-olds do not play with older children in the sense of sharing toys and ideas, it is healthy for them to be with their peers. Children who spend all of their time with giant adults miss the opportunity of relating to people their own size. Because of the strength of their instincts and the small size of their sense of self and inner conscience, toddlers are unable to share their toys. In other words, they are normally selfish. By playing with peers with adult supervision, toddlers will eventually learn to share their possessions.

Meanwhile, the emotional tape is eternally recording. We will explain, further on, just what part this mental recording plays in a person's relationships.

During these difficult years of mastery, a creative child may invent a special kind of transitional object—an imaginary companion. This invisible pal cannot be shared with anyone else, is always accepting of the toddler's behavior, and is readily available for all sorts of conversations. The imaginary companion can easily be blamed for broken vases, spilled sugar, or bashed dogs. Some toddlers invest their teddy bears, animals, and even trees with all-accepting mother characteristics. Such creative thinking should be encouraged, as it indicates that special coping resources have begun to develop. It is not a sign of insanity, as many adults think.

The adult residues of the anal phase of psychosexual development should be an ability to share responsibilities, a desire for cleanliness, a generous nature, an ability to overcome frustration through reason, and a sense of orderliness about one's life. If the parents have been too rigid and controlling during the toddler period, the children can become fixated at this stage of development. These unfortunate people may be stubborn, unwilling and unable to give love or even favors to others, miserly about their money and possessions, petty about minute details, and obsessed either with cleanliness or sloppiness.

If they received continually mixed messages from their parents, they may develop obsessional thinking patterns which interfere with mature decision-making. The obsessive person thinks like this: "I think I'll read a book, but maybe I'd better go shopping. On the other hand, there's a good TV show on, but maybe I should be washing the car." The end result is that the obsessive person doesn't get anything done, having used up excessive energy in ruminative thought.

The infant and toddler stages are governed by a loving, highly dependent attachment to the mother. This mother love is of a highly sensualized nature. In the first months there is the body contact during feeding time. Enough has been said about the sucking pleasure. Then there is the sensual arousal experienced while the mother bathes and changes the child. That really feels good. Then the mother directs the children's interest to their genitals during bowel and bladder training. She teaches the toddling boy to hold his penis and the little girl and boy to wipe themselves. These maternal duties help to form and solidify the erotic attachment between mother and child.

Chapter **5**

The Preschool and School Years

FROM BABY INTO CHILD

between the ages of two and three toddlers become preschool children. They now begin the often difficult task of relinquishing the sensualized attachment to mother. They must free their energies to invest in activities and in people beyond the family, especially in peers. Nature dictates that children eventually become autonomous of the nurturing parent. Children have a great psychological force toward independence, which is exemplified by their quest for self-assertion during the toddler phase.

Some mothers cannot bear to see their little children become independent little people. A part of them enjoys the baby's helpless stages; and so, without being aware of it, they exert a regressive pull against the child's forward movement. This pull can be seen in continuing nursing beyond the appropriate weaning time and in giving milk or candy to a child experiencing normal frustration. These oral regressive pulls imprint onto the child's unconscious: "You can solve everything by drinking or eating. Don't learn any further coping devices."

57

The regressive parent can inhibit the child's growth by excessively delaying bowel training, discouraging exploration and curiosity, treating the outside world as a fearful place, and having a permissive attitude about rules and controls. Such a mother is actually satisfying her own unfulfilled infantile needs through her child. We label this kind of adult a "child-mother." Her need to infantilize her child extends to other people in her environment. These anal-regressive pulls at this stage imprint on the child's emotional memory tape that it's better to stay by mother's side rather than to venture forth.

The average mother is relieved to see a baby become a child, for the infantile dependency period is exhausting to a parent, both physically and emotionally. It is a great responsibility to hold a child's life in one's hands. In addition, children are self-destructive to the extent that they have no conception of injury or death. What a relief to have them take over at least partial responsibility for their own survival.

GENDER-IDENTITY PERIOD

Between three and six, the child's tasks become the giving up of the mother, establishing his or her sexual identity, and preparing for the outside world. These tasks are complicated, requiring further gentle and sometimes frustrating prodding from the mother and the support of the father in validating the child as a unique person. This phase is called the *gender-identity period*. We can no longer lump boys and girls in the same category during these preschool years. The gender-identity period is quite different for the sexes, and not just culturally either.

In our past discussion we did not mean to leave the father on the sidelines. The father's love is very important to the baby and toddler. In our society, however, he is usually a secondary bonding figure because he is most often absent from the home during the major part of an infant's or toddler's day. The nurturing parent with the major childcare responsibilities naturally has a more profound impact on the young personality. Some men still have a difficult time relating to babies, and wait until the child is three or more to establish a consistent relationship.

We will explain the identity journey of boys first because their development is not so complex as that of little girls.

The male child's first love is heterosexual. His first identification is with his mother, since she is the adult who is most often present. The goal of his gender-identity period is to switch identities from feminine to masculine. Every human has a mixture of the male and female within him, both physically and mentally. One sexual identity usually emerges to dominate a person's sense of gender.

Around three, or soon after bowel training, the erotic zone moves from the anal area to the genital area. Since the little boy loves his mother, he associates his new pleasurable genital sensations with her. He also has the earlier memory of those wonderful baths.

The little boy is *very* emotionally attached to his penis. He takes great delight in urinating from it and in touching it. Masturbation, erections, and the pleasurable sensations associated with his penis are nature's ways of pulling him toward adult sexuality.

During the gender-identity period, boys develop longings for and plans to marry their mother. The father is experienced as a fierce competitor for mother's exclusive attention. The mother's role is again that of the gentle frustrator. The little boy must learn to give up his emotional claims on the mother in order to grow up. The father should be emotionally prepared to teach the boy the positive aspects of being male.

Sometimes the regressive mother does not desire her miniature husband to grow up. Sometimes the father is ineffectual, or he is disinterested in his son's development and rejects the little boy's attempts to learn male identification. The stepfather who enters a family with this problem will have to break up this emotionally unhealthy mother attachment. Neither mother nor child may be grateful for the attempt.

In the normal family the little boy becomes somewhat fearful of his father. After all, the huge adult may suspect that the little fellow has murderous wishes toward him. Children think in strange and magical ways. Big Daddy could easily kill him, the little boy may reason. In most instances, the child fears that the father might harm his most precious body possession, his penis. The child may be unaware of this fear, but may experience nightmares involving animals chasing him or monsters wielding knives.

Between the years of three and five the little boy gives up his desires to be like his mother or to have her to himself. The gradual shift in identities is rarely smooth. The parents' patience is greatly tested during this period as the little boy bounces back and forth in his identities, one day being like mother, the next day like father. Peer pressure, as well as the father's wishes for his son to establish his male identity, encourage the little boy to leave his mother's side.

Unfortunately, our cultural attitudes prescribe that a boy must renounce all of that normal part of his psyche which is considered female. That is, his intuitive gifts become suppressed, and he is trained to think logically. His gentleness is encouraged to be covered up and replaced with toughness. The only males in our society who can be obviously gentle are doctors, hair stylists, or masseurs. Boys are taught not to cry, to be highly competitive, and to consider women as inferior objects. All these attitudes are cultural and not natural.

Even though sexist attitudes have been exposed through the efforts of the women's liberation movement, old attitudes die hard. The reality of our society is that the majority of children are still reared in a sexist atmosphere. These societal behavioral rules are imprinted on the boy's unconscious, along with whatever familial treatment he receives.

During the gender-identity phase, the little boy may

make several different identifications with male figures other than his father. An older brother, a close uncle, a grandfather, or a family friend may be influential in shaping the boy's sense of gender.

The little girl's first relationship in life is homosexual. She loves her mother with the same intensity as does the little boy. During her gender-identity period, she does not have to switch identifications as does the boy. She experiences the father as an intruder, because the little girl also desires the mother's exclusive attention. The normal mother frustrates the little girl's wishes, thus pushing the female toward heterosexuality. The daughter becomes the miniature woman during these years and is in open competition for the father's love and attention. Many mothers admit that this period in their daughter's life is the most trying and upsetting.

Little girls are fiercely jealous of their mother's time with and affection for the father. But mothers can also be jealous of their daughter's closer relationship with the man of the house. Sometimes, particularly if the man and woman are having problems, the father actually prefers his little girl to his wife.

The little girl must eventually lose this contest if she is to grow up and eventually find a man of her own. If she wins the contest, she will become fixated at this stage and spend her adult years seeking a sugar daddy. The father's role is to show acceptance of the little girl with appropriate praise and affection. However, he must get the message across that she must give him up, identify again with her mother, and eventually leave home to find her own man.

Sometimes fathers feel sexually aroused by their daughter's seductive behavior. If they are unaware that these erotic feelings are normal, some fathers feel guilty. They may even think the child is at fault and put down her budding femininity. This harsh rejection can be devastating to a little girl's sense of worth as a female.

The parents' attitudes about maleness and femaleness are all-important for the child's self-view. If the mother enjoys her life as a female, the daughter will too. She learns her values from the mother as she models herself in the mother's image. What she learns, positive or negative, becomes part of her overall sense of self.

In the female-gendering years, the young girl experiences two rejections, one from mother and one from father. The male child has only one rejection to contend with, but then he must make a change in the object of his identification. Each sex has it own complexities and proves the point that it's hard to be a child, and even harder to grow up.

During the gender-identity phase, children greatly increase their coping skills. Preschool children begin to deal with infantile jealousy by trying to earn attention through appropriate behavior rather than by pouting or whining. They become more active than passive during peer play. Also their patience develops further. They learn to share possessions, for they begin to understand and accept the notion that the parents must be shared with others. The world is greatly expanded for preschoolers as they venture into new groups of children, relations, and nursery-school peers.

Children who become emotionally autonomous from their mothers are ready to enter school. Children see themselves as separate persons if they have successfully resolved strivings for the opposite-sex parent. Energies are freed to learn in school and to develop friendships.

This widening circle of new people in their lives can be quite surprising to some children. A child's family patterns are, to him or her, the way of the world. To discover that other families behave differently can cause a youngster confusion. This is most obvious when two families merge in remarriage. Resiliency, however, is part of human nature, and the majority of children absorb new information with ease and thus enrich their lives. After all, just because the folks eat only meat and potatoes doesn't mean that fish and garlic are bad.

LATENCY PERIOD

By the age of six, the child's emotional memory tape is loaded with information. Erotic attachments to parents are consciously suppressed, but will definitely be a determining factor in later love choices.

From seven to eleven (or whenever puberty begins), children are in a latency period. That is, their attachments to their parents are somewhat lessened or at least less obvious. In the school years, children's interests are directed toward peer acceptance and approval, mastering social skills, learning in school, hobbies, and athletic achievements. Each success in the above-mentioned areas adds to the child's self-esteem and sense of independence.

Although the children's consciences are not yet fully formed, they no longer have the ever-present parents to tell them right from wrong. Other adults supervise their behavior during the day. Peer pressures, either positive or negative, become incorporated into schoolchildren's system of inner justice. Society at large, through the media, education, and religious training, is very influential during the latency period.

We feel that, during the school years, children learn a certain negative lesson about emotions and the expression of feelings. In our culture affectionate touching is frowned upon. School-age children soon learn that the affection they were raised with is somehow not correct. Physical contact is acceptable in sports, but nowhere else. This cold attitude increases the boys-against-girls orientation and disrupts any natural, affectionate relationships or friendships between the sexes. It also affects people's adult relationships in a limiting and tragic way; for few men and women enjoy opposite-sex friends in a relationship that has affection as an integral part of it. This is a psychological loss for adults, because affectionate friends of both sexes enrich one's life.

Chapter **6**

The Adolescent Years

The child's latency period ends with the new spurt of hormonal and physical growth that announces puberty. The carefree child quickly becomes the preoccupied adolescent. Many adults have memories of their grade-school days, but have amnesia about their early teenage years. The reason for this memory lapse is that puberty is the most painful of all the developmental stages. It is also painful for the parents, and especially so for stepparents.

THRUST TOWARD AUTONOMY

During the teenage years young people must make a final break from dependency on their families. Healthy autonomy is what adolescence is all about. In poor societies, teenagers leave home early because of financial reasons. In affluent societies, teenagers are expected to remain financially dependent on parents until young adulthood, especially if they are in the process of finishing an extended education. This dependency tends to keep adolescents in a regressed state of half-child and half-adult. Despite the fact that this situation is very common, it is definitely not healthy.

Some parents cannot accept the independent spirit of their teenagers and try to stop their growth. They seem to forget that the parental job is to rear children so that they can leave home and enter society as their own persons. We do not own our children, nor can we protect them from the reality of the world they must enter.

The transition years from juvenile to young adult are psychologically difficult. Adolescents reexperience and must resolve the original developmental stages. Teenagers do not reexperience these phases in succession, as do infants, but all at once. They have the additional burden of dealing with an instinctual surge of sexuality and aggression, nature's message that it is time to form a new family and find one's own niche in the world of work. However, society's message is quite different, and teenagers are artificially forced to be dependent on parents.

Always hungry and profusely talkative, at least among themselves, teenagers are reexperiencing oral drives. The adolescent's romance with dirt is symbolic of the anal period. The aggressive renunciation of parental views bespeaks an identity crisis relating to the earlier unresolved gender-identity needs.

When teenagers expound on radical ideas which put down parental views, they are only proclaiming that they are separate people, different from their parents. At this time parents have long ago solidified their opinions and viewpoints about religion, politics, and the world at large. Parents assume that the teenagers are also solidifying their philosophies of life. They are doing nothing of the kind. They are simply taking opposite viewpoints in order to widen the space in their search for independence.

As an example we are reminded of one of our teenagers announcing her decision to become a vegetarian. Along with this declaration came the proclamation that we were all on the verge of cannibalism as the rest of the family were meat-eaters. At such a point, parents must decide what tack they will take: pay attention to the insult and become defensive, put down or ridicule the teenager's new practice, or give the teenager the opportunity to be different.

We encouraged our daughter to read up on correct diet, on vitamin needs, and on how to obtain whole proteins from vegetables alone. Since we were busy with our practices and with rearing four other children, she had to take responsibility for her own cooking. We suggested she eat in her room if she was offended by our menu. The other children were told to leave their sister alone and not to tease her about her choice of foods.

Our daughter diligently studied her new diet and cooked her meals "her way"—for about three weeks. Then, one night, she drifted back to the dinner table to join the rest of the family. No one teased her or made her lose face. If we had made a big deal out of her decision, she would have felt forced to keep up her new habits after she had lost interest. We let her be herself while not allowing her ideas to infringe upon our life style.

Teenagers love and need to be involved in projects, as such activity channels some of their intense aggression, which otherwise might be directed at themselves or at their parents. If parents can be flexible, they can even learn from a searching teenager. One of our boys, at sixteen, declared that he was leaving school. He was going to study with a guru and we would probably never see him again. He was determined. As we were raised in the "complete your school, get a job" culture, our first thoughts ran along the lines of, "Oh, my God! He'll never finish school!" On second thought, we suggested he request a leave of absence, travel to his guru (on his own money), and see if this kind of life was to his liking.

He was gone for four months. An occasional postcard let us know he was alive and well. When he did return, he shared his knowledge with us and gave us valuable tools for increasing one's well-being. Thus we all profited from our son's trial at independence.

If teenagers cannot find opposite viewpoints about which to argue, they will seek to diminish their parents' physical characteristics. The once idealized parent seems to develop disgusting mannerisms such as making nerve-grating sounds while chewing and swallowing food. As a stepparent you will probably receive less of this disdain since you were most likely never idealized in the first place.

One of our teenagers was studying his father quite intently one evening. Suddenly he said, "Oh, grossness! Look at your leg veins!" "So what?" replied his Dad. "They're so big!" said the son. "That makes me a bad guy," said Dad, who had already gone through this "put-down" routine with two previous adolescents. Both of them started to laugh at the son's obvious intent to de-idealize his father.

During these personal-attack years parents must keep in mind the psychological motivation behind this unpleasant process. The motivation is, "I'm me and you're you, and I want to be different." Bright teenagers will often be absolutely correct in their comments about parental faults. No sense getting super-defensive, since no one is perfect anyway.

One fourteen-year-old boy complained how tough his father was when the boy got in trouble. We asked him whom he would prefer for a father. After much thought he said, "Why someone like Santa Claus, of course." Our question helped him to understand that he wanted everything his own way and that this expectation was unreasonable.

While the importance of parental influence is being deemphasized, teenagers throw their allegiance in strange directions. Again this is a natural attempt to become independent from parents. Sudden crushes on movie or singing stars can envelop a teenager with ferocious absorption. Friends become all-important, with a cloak of secrecy thrown over conversations when parents are present. It is hard for parents not to feel jealous and rejected by suddenly becoming third-rate citizens in the eyes of people who just yesterday attributed God-like qualities to them. If parents can keep a light attitude and concentrate more on their marriage relationship, then teenage attacks will lose their impact on self-esteem. Parents must also keep in mind that teenagers are leery of all adults; parents and stepparents are not their sole targets.

INTERNAL CONFLICT

Teenagers are overly sensitive to other's remarks, highly egocentric, and vacillating in their opinions. They have so much internal conflict during these years that they have little energy left for consideration or thoughtfulness.

Teenagers have an active fantasy life centering around sexuality and aggression. Most feel guilty about their fantasies and seek punishment from their parents or other authority figures. They are not aware of their wish for punishment, however. Thus their guilt provokes strange behavior, such as constant twitchings, nervous tappings, inability to look parents in the eye, hair twisting, nail biting, and constant interruptions of adult discussions. It's a drag for all concerned.

During the teenage years, stepchildren are by far the most difficult to handle. Stepparents should remind themselves that *all* adolescents, even if they are natural children, are mostly impossible miniadults. Adult self-confidence is essential when rearing teenagers. In their attempts to become themselves, adolescents must attack adult systems. If the parents take these attacks personally, they remove the testing ground for the rebellious adolescents.

It is best to allow them to state *their* opinions in an accepting atmosphere.*

The adolescent must also learn about love and intimacy. Relating to the opposite sex becomes a primary concern for teenagers, and suddenly they don't know how. Bodily changes, instinctual sex drives, and peer pressures and attitudes must be absorbed and integrated into the teenagers' sense of their new self. No wonder, then, that adolescents have such a need for privacy to sort out the variety of feelings that bombard them daily.

It is well to remember that teenagers eventually do grow up and leave the nest. Many a parent wishes that that would occur sooner than it does. These wishes are perfectly normal, for it is hard to live with self-centered teenagers.

The entire organization of the personality does not come together until the middle twenties. It is at this time that both children and stepchildren can become friends with the parents. After all those years of childcare, the parental reward can be a sense of deep accomplishment. Stepparents may feel even more esteem than the natural parent because of the corrective parenting they may have done.

All information that has been imprinted upon the emotional tape of young adults will begin to affect their life choices. This process is called *repetition compulsion*. The unconscious seeks to find people and situations that will be familiar to it. Thus adults who were unloved children will be drawn to pick unloving partners. Such choices make the adult consciously miserable but keep the unconscious satisfied. At the same time, the unloved child who received corrective love from a stepparent will have had the original emotional tape erased and a new message imprinted. The adolescent years, because of the revival and resolution of the early developmental stages, provide a second chance for parents to undo and repair original errors.

*See Part III, Chapter 9, pages 106-108 for guidelines on communicating with teenagers.

PART **III**

*STEPPARENTING PROBLEMS
AND REWARDS*

Chapter **7**

Instant Family—
Expectations and Reality

BEST INTENTIONS CAN FAIL

Jim married Elsa after a brief, intensely romantic courtship. He felt very protective of Elsa and her eleven-year-old daughter, Nancy. He was going to make up to them for all the years they had suffered at the hands of an alcoholic brute. Jim fantasized that Nancy would be grateful for his paternal concern. Nancy, however, had been so traumatized by her real father's drinking and his beatings of her and her mother, that she wanted nothing to do with Jim, or any other male.

She had pleaded with Elsa before the wedding to "please keep everything the way it was before him." Elsa knew that Jim was a kind and gentle man and that Nancy would eventually learn to love him. Elsa also was wise enough to know she couldn't let her daughter's wishes stand in the way of her own happiness.

Nancy, a bright young girl, invented a system for rejecting Jim or any of his overtures of friendship. At dinnertime she refused to answer even simple questions, ate noisily, and seemed to be intentionally rude. She would usually start crying over nothing and storm away to her room. One day Jim and Elsa came home from work and found all of Jim's clothes in the front yard. Nancy would acknowledge Jim's presence only with the phrase "Oh, Ick's here."

No one was prepared for the next event that occurred. Elsa's older daughter, Sally, arrived on the doorstep announcing her impending divorce. She moved in, bringing her unhappiness with her luggage. During the seven years since Elsa's divorce, the girls had received her undivided attention and thus took it for granted. Sally, now in need of mothering again, did not take too kindly to this stranger named Jim.

Jim tried to help Sally and was soundly rebuffed. All his dreams of being the rescuing father figure were rapidly dissolving. Elsa, trying to keep everyone happy, found herself wondering if she'd made a bad choice of a mate. Every time Jim walked into a room occupied by the two daughters, he was the recipient of hateful looks. Being a patient man, he lowered his expectations and finally left them alone. The emotional vibes in the home were terrible.

This stand-off solution left everyone tense. The situation was getting worse by the day, despite Jim's well-intentioned retreat. Nancy's sullenness, Sally's hostility, and Jim's stoic acceptance of their hate finally got to Elsa.

One morning, while preparing breakfast, Elsa took a realistic look at her daughters. Jim had already left for work. Both girls were grumbling about inconsequential matters. The usually mild-mannered Elsa spoke up: "Sally, you can leave today. You're a grown woman, acting like a baby. You have no thought in your head for me, my marriage, or my happiness. So, either get some help for yourself or kindly get out."

"You, Nancy, are a spoiled brat. No matter how nastily you behave, you cannot make me stop loving Jim. You will stop using the word 'Ick.' You will eat in your room if you can't behave. The time of coddling is over! Also, fix your own damn breakfast!" With that said, Elsa marched out of the kitchen, feeling better than she had in weeks. Her embarrassed daughters were left at the table, stunned by Elsa's proclamations.

This "dynamite" approach goes against all the lovely books and articles that advise people about the art of talking over problems. In reality, such step-by-step approaches, kindness on everyone's part, and letting the youngsters have equal time don't always succeed. Those instructions have an aura of phoniness about them. They surely are not designed for people who show such infantile behavior as Nancy and Sally. How does one reason with a pouting, self-centered eleven-year-old? Most normal parents react with anger.

Elsa's explosion rocked Sally back to reality. She sat down with her mother and apologized for intruding in her marriage. She also realized that in her own anguish she had never even taken the time to consider Jim's feelings, nor had she bothered to get to know him. Sally said, "I guess I just wanted you to be good old Mom, always waiting at home to take care of me. I really felt jealous that you had someone whom you loved, but I was all alone."

Sally did seek counseling and learned that her immediate hatred of Jim was actually stored-up anger she felt for her soon-to-be-ex-husband. She moved out of her mother's home and established her own apartment. When she visits Jim and Elsa now, she arrives as a welcomed guest rather than as a spoiled brat in an adult disguise. Sally has learned to enjoy knowing that her mother is finally a fulfilled and happy woman, thanks to Jim's love.

Nancy had actually grown bored with the game she was playing against Jim. Secretly she knew he was a nice guy. She had needed her mother's firm announcement to reshape her reality. Before Jim's arrival, she hadn't really been that involved with Elsa anyway. Friends, music lessons, skiing, and horseback riding were her main interests, the usual preoccupations of most young girls. Her rejection game with Jim had come to absorb more and more of her free time.

Nancy didn't suddenly like or love Jim, but she did stop antagonizing him. The air was cleared. Elsa regained control of her life, and she and Jim resumed their romantic feelings. Love needs a serene atmosphere in which to flourish.

It took Jim and Nancy over a year to become entirely comfortable with each other. Everyone learned something valuable. Jim now advises new stepparents to expect children to feel bumped aside, their prominent positions in a one-parent family instantly usurped by an adult.

Time, usually two years, is required for all members of the family to make the necessary adjustments. Elsa talks about not letting children overwhelm you with their reactions. "You can identify with their feelings too much and forget you have a life too," states a contented Elsa. Nancy isn't a spoiled brat anymore. She likes herself better now because, underneath all their misbehavior, children don't enjoy being hateful. Sally has learned to relate to her mother as a person with her own needs, not just as an unselfish, all-giving Mom.

BE FLEXIBLE, EXPECT THE WORST

The novice parent joining an existing family unit must enter armed with flexibility; for this group of people has been living together for many years with established patterns. Some of these patterns may appear weird—and may very well be. The younger the children are, the easier it is for them to accept a new parent figure. All children vary in their ability to accept change. Generally speaking, however, the adolescent has the most difficult time adjusting to a stepparent. In Part II you read about normal childhood development. Understanding the stages of normal emotional growth from infancy through adolescence will help you contend with the idiosyncrasies of new stepchildren.

As a new stepparent, you should expect that the children will be jealous of you. If you assume that dealing with children's envy will be a part of your daily life, then it will not be such a shock when little Sue insists on sitting between you and your new mate. This jealousy abates as the child begins to accept your presence as routine and actually starts to receive some emotional benefits from you.

One stepfather told us that he was amazed at the tactics his stepchild used in order to set up conflicts between him and his wife. One evening he was peacefully reading the paper when Kim, age fourteen, came waltzing through the living room in bikini pants and bra. He told her to put on her clothes. She shrieked "Rapist!" and ran for the kitchen to get Mom. Luckily, the mother had heard the whole scene. She calmly marched Kim upstairs. Through her tears Kim confessed she wanted Dad back home. Maybe if she told everyone that her stepfather was a child molester, Dad would come home again.

One would think a fourteen-year-old could understand the realities of life better. Dad had remarried; Mom had remarried. However, the reunion of the original parents is the most commonly held fantasy of the children of divorce. It is a normal fantasy because human beings do not like change, particularly when it involves family.

As a new stepparent you must have the expectation that you may be treated as a temporary guest for quite some time. Even if you feel you have established good rapport with the children before the marriage, do not assume your new role as stepparent will be welcomed overnight.

If you enter an established family, do not expect gratitude for taking on such heavy responsibilities. You may be a great financial asset, a super repairman/cook/entertainer, but the normally self-centered child will show no gratitude. Well, the child may show a little, but don't count on it.

Expectations of stepparenting should be based on reality. Looking realistically is difficult for many people because they are in love with their partners. We all idealize those we love and imagine that, because we love, everything will be easy. However, falling in love is just the beginning of a relationship. With children already present, that glow of love will be impinged upon again and again.

The stepparent should expect that the children will relate to him or her as a single, foreign unit. That is, in a natural family the children see Mom and Dad as a combined force, two people who respond as one. Since the stepchildren have lived with and depended upon one parent for some time, it is difficult for them to picture the parent with another partner. They will automatically exclude the stepparent from decisions they must work through. They will ask the natural parent for food, money, or favors as if the stepparent were nonexistent. You must realize that this is normal and to be expected.

Just because your new mate trusts you emotionally does not mean that the children will follow suit. You will have to earn their trust just as you would in an adult friendship. You can earn this trust by being emotionally consistent. Being consistent will be difficult, as you are also going to have to understand and accept their resentments, jealousies, and rejections. We have found that if stepparents can learn to step back a bit and *not take things personally*, they will help lighten the atmosphere.

How can you remain unmoved when Johnny is asking you, "When are you leaving? Isn't it time for you to go to your own home now?" Or when little Penny throws out a delightful tidbit like, "You're not as handsome (pretty) as my real Dad (Mom)." It is possible to be objective about children's hostilities if you understand that their anger and resentments are *normal*; also that these feelings are not aimed at you as a person but are meant for the situation. You'll help the children and yourself if you can maintain a sense of humor during these trying times of original adjustment to a new mother or father.

Keep in mind that your new marriage must be given a chance in order to be rewarding. The demands of rearing any children are great. Parents deserve and need private times together. Establish such a quiet time every day. Try to get away for a weekend every few weeks. Often stepchildren leave to visit their natural parent, providing you and your loved one a chance to enjoy each other alone.

ONE FAMILY, TWO STEPPARENTS

Some remarriages involve two sets of children, so that both adults have to learn to be stepparents together. All the problems of parenting are doubled. Siblings, even if they don't like each other, have grown up around one another. Suddenly four or five kids get plopped together and must cope with each other. The most difficult adjustment is having suddenly to share one's territory. If the man moves into the woman's home with his belongings and children, room must be made for them. Can you imagine having to share your room with a stranger?

Most couples cannot afford to buy a new home to accommodate the expanded family. The noise level doubles. The household chores increase tremendously. Everyone looks for his or her special place in the new blend of two families. Since children feel more secure in structured situations, family conferences can be held to let all members know what their duties will be. Family rules should be explained so that everyone knows what is expected.

Anticipate that the mixture of children will be chaotic for a while, perhaps a year or two. Do not assume that the children will like each other, or make them feel guilty if they pronounce their hatred. Both parents should discuss a plan of benign neglect when children's fights are involved. Unless murder seems imminent, let the kids thrash out their own problems, as all peers must do. If the stepparents get overly involved with petty disagreements, the children will never learn to work things out themselves. Besides, it is far too easy to fall into that nonsensical game of "my kids" and "your monsters."

Visiting stepchildren can also be stressful for a family.
John has two sons, Bob, seven, and Ned, five, who visit
him every other weekend, at Christmas, and for two
months in the summer. The boys have a stepfather, "Mr.
Joe," whom they hate. John is married to Felicia, who was
a widow with a son, Larry, six, and a daughter, Melinda,
four. Quite a crowd of people every other weekend and at
holiday time! The situation has all the makings of a zoo.
Both adults enjoyed children, so having four little ones
around the apartment didn't bother John or Felicia. The
problem was that John's boys wanted to come and live with
him. They felt jealous of Larry and Melinda because those
two kids had the boys' father all the time.

The parents made sure that Bob and Ned felt they had a
second home. There was a bedroom just for them, stocked
with their clothes and toys. Felicia and John changed the
subject whenever the boys brought up the fact that they
could not live with Dad. Being little kids, they soon forgot
the question. Young children have no conception of what
custody means. Thus, further explanation would just be
confusing. However, this diversionary tactic will backfire
with older children.

John and Felicia also understood that they were the
"visited" parents, with whom everything seemed like fun
and games. "Mr. Joe" was a nice man who did not mistreat
his stepsons. He did have to do the day-to-day disciplining,
however. So, of course, things looked better at Dad's
house. Instead of taking his children's wishes to live with
him as an ego trip, John looked at the reality of the differ-
ence between the playtime parent and the everyday parent.

THE EX-MATE WON'T DISAPPEAR

Another aspect of stepparenting is dealing with your
husband's or wife's first mate, the other natural parent of
your stepchildren. Ex-mates do not suddenly disappear
when you marry someone else. It's a rare, mature "ex"

who wishes happiness for the previous mate's second marriage. How would you feel if your husband divorced you, left you with the kids, lived it up as a swinging bachelor, and then married a woman ten years younger than yourself? You would most likely feel vindictive toward your ex and his new partner.

When visiting his father and stepmother, Mike, age seven, would always seem to disappear when it was time to eat; or he would announce that he wasn't hungry. If he did eat, he seemed to examine and compare everyone's plate with his own. As Mike had always been a hearty eater in the past, this behavior was very strange. Come to find out, through Dad's ex-sister-in-law, Mike's mother had told the boy that his new stepmother was going to poison him!

Incredible as it may sound, it's a true story. The ex-sister-in-law couldn't believe her ears and felt obligated to inform the father. Mike and his father had a long talk about how scared the little fellow had been. Stepmother then reassured Mike that she would never hurt him, gave him some cuddling, and treated the entire matter as casually as possible.

The original marital partner can also attempt to make the newly married person feel guilty about his or her new life, especially if the newlywed seems happy. The previous mate can send pitiful messages using the children as carriers of woe: "Mom says we can't go to camp this summer because you don't give her enough money"—as Dad fidgets, trying to control his temper, mentally adding up the $300 he pays out every month. Stepmother, who works to keep them above water, fumes, thinking about the sacrifices they all make because of the child-support payments he must meet.

There is no sense in becoming defensive with children when they relay kinfe-jab messages from your ex. It's not the child's fault, and the youngster probably doesn't want to hear any lengthy explanations. You can stand up for equal time when the youngsters become late adolescents, around seventeen. If they still feel you mistreated Mom or Dad, you can give them all the facts and let them decide for themselves. You should also take care not to send overly happy messages back to your ex-partner. Doing that can only generate anger and jealousy for which you surely will pay.

As a stepparent you should expect that your new mate will have to spend some of his or her time communicating with the first mate. It will probably seem like *too* much time and effort, no matter how little or how much effort is actually expended. Be patient and recognize that some of the communicating is done out of guilt. Remember that you are receiving the vast majority of the attention that your partner has to give.

Some parents try to maintain a pleasant relationship with an ex-spouse out of fear. The fear is that the rejected mate may emotionally harm the children. Some resentful ex-partners wield great power by nit-picking over "reasonable visitation rights." Reasonable to whom? Whoever has custody will probably decide what is reasonable.

One couple we know spends two months out of the year placating and generally being too nice to the husband's ex-wife in order to persuade her to let his daughters visit for three days after Christmas. The natural mother thinks she is perfectly reasonable. If the father and stepmother put too much pressure on this lady, she begins to think out loud that the daughters' three-week summer visit with Dad was bad.

In the process, her daughters have learned to hate her. They are very aware that Mom doesn't want them to love their Dad. Her withholding attitude about visits to Dad only increases the girls' longing to see their father more often. When the father told us of this dilemma, we predicted that the girls would eventually run away from home. Sure enough, on their last visit they both talked about future escape plans. Visitation, as we shall detail later in the book,* should be determined by what best fulfills the needs of all concerned, rather than by a legal decree.

If his ex-wife hassles him, your new husband needs a great deal of emotional support from you. Your new wife needs encouragement and care if her ex-mate lays heavy guilt trips on her. All parents who leave their children miss the experience of watching them achieve and grow from day to day. So be gentle with your mate if he or she misses the children. Nor should you mistake the longing to see the children for missing the first marital partner.

GUILTS AND JEALOUSIES

Some parents feel guilty if they have left their own children and become stepparents for other children. They may hold back affection and attention from their stepchildren because they feel guilty about deserting their own. The best medicine for this malaise is talking about the feelings with someone who cares. A competent psychotherapist is essential if these feelings cannot be worked out between the two partners themselves.

Guilt is the most meaningless of all feelings. Feeling guilty doesn't change any situation for the better. If you can do something about a situation, then do it. If you are powerless to change some aspects of your life, forget it. Invest your energies in positive acts and feelings rather than in guilt. Guilty feelings just decrease a person's self-esteem. Guilt is a worthless commodity inherited from one's parents. It never helps.

One wife who felt that her husband had deserted her for a younger woman would have the children telephone their father and ask plaintively, "Why don't you come over and see us more often, Daddy?" Actually, the ex-wife

*See Part III, Chapter 11, pages 135-136.

wanted his attention so that she could cry on his shoulder about how painful life had been since he left. When he came to visit the children, she shooed them away and began to act seductively toward her ex-husband. His new wife suggested that perhaps he was only visiting to alleviate his guilt. She suggested that he pick up the children and take them for a ride, or bring them over to his new home.

Since their mother always referred to the new wife as "that woman," the children never thought of her as a second mother, but rather as someone they should hate. "That woman" happened to be a very kind and loving person who made great efforts to let the children know she liked them. Naturally affectionate, she casually hugged and kissed them whenever they came to visit. The children gradually relaxed to the point of calling her Aunty Laurie. Someday they'll be able to experience her as their second mother and perhaps eventually as their real psychological mother.

Some stepparents feel jealous if the original parents let bygones be bygones and become friends. Ex-mates sometimes like to reminisce about past pleasant experiences and travels, and also about the time when the children were babies. As a stepparent, you can feel excluded if your spouse and his or her ex-mate reminisce in the presence of their mutual children. Accept the fact that you were not a part of the past. All past marriages were not horrendous one hundred percent of the time. Keep in mind that your mate loves you now. Continued intense hatred of an ex-mate uses emotional energy that could be directed positively toward yourself. Remember that it's beneficial to the children to discover that divorced parents are capable of being friends again.

We hope we don't sound too negative about the reactions you can expect from stepchildren. If remarriage were a simple adjustment for everyone concerned, there would be no need for a book on successful stepparenting.

Keep in mind that it takes at least a year for newly married childless couples to adjust to one another. Surely it makes sense that couples with children will need a longer period of time to work out the emotional adjustments of new family mixes.

Chapter 8

Problems and Solutions

DISCIPLINING HURDLES

Child-discipline procedures seem to be the most formidable problem between natural parents and stepparents. Some second parents feel timid about punishing their stepchildren and leave everything to the natural parent. Some natural parents resent any interference by the stepparent. The children have been relating to one authority figure for some time, and usually balk at a stepparent's disciplinary tactics.

Questions about the type of punishment, who should be in charge, and what constitutes bad behavior should be answered before the marriage. Since the majority of lovers shy away from this sticky issue, they can end up in some royal battles in their daily lives after the marriage.

Every stepparent will relate to the following anecdote, for it will have happened to him in one form or another. The family is in the car. Dad and step-Mom are in the front seat, the two kids in back. The kids start to fight. Step-Mom looks to their Dad to check whether he's going to stop them. Since he does nothing, step-Mom turns around and says, "Stop it! Right now!" The kids quit their fight, but one or the other state vehemently, "You can't tell me what to do. You're not my real mother!" Stepmother feels rejected. Dad doesn't know what to say. The kids are upset. A great beginning for a lousy day.

Some unsure stepparents actually believe the rejecting statements of the stepchild. Consider that a schoolteacher or a policeman also are not "real" parents; however, they and many other authority figures tell children how to behave in a given day. All adults are potential instructors for children. A stepparent is just as adult as the natural parent. The best answer to the real-parent challenge is, "It doesn't matter; your real Mom (Dad) wouldn't want you to fight either"; or, "I'm your second Mom (Dad) and have the say-so in this house."

This approach clearly informs the child that you are an authority to be reckoned with. If a natural parent refuses to share the role of disciplinarian, the stepparent is reduced to a child's position without power. The child in such a lopsided arrangement tends to disrespect the stepparent and to view him or her as just another child. Both parents must be authority figures, never just one.

Karen had been married twice. Both of her husbands were unstable men. Her first was a drug addict, the second a wife-beater. Neither of the men was responsible enough to hold a job very long. Karen always worked and was a very independent lady. She had lived with her nine-year-old son, just the two of them, for four years. She vowed to her friends that she would never consider marrying again.

That vow was broken when she met David. He was sweet, caring, and a successful attorney. They married after a few months. Before the wedding, however, David noticed that whenever he reprimanded her little boy, Joey, Karen would glare at him. Trying to maintain the romantic illusion, the couple never actually talked about Joey's discipline. He certainly needed some shaping up. Joey was always overstepping his bounds. He sassed adults, interrupted them at will, and refused to obey orders.

Karen and David's first big fight occurred after the second week of marriage. David had already reared four boys, so he was a well-experienced father. He saw Joey making mudballs and inserting rocks in the center of the missiles. Just as Joey heaved the first mudball at a passing car, David grabbed him, gave him a good smack on the behind, and ordered him to his room. Karen came running out of the house and told Joey to go to his friend's house instead. She effectively reduced David's adult position to zero. This scene set the stage for some seemingly unresolvable conflicts.

The couple entered marriage counseling. After much defensive rationalizing, Karen learned the disservice she was doing to Joey's development. Unconsciously, Karen believed that all men were incompetent and not to be trusted. She transferred this negative attitude onto David and thus interfered with his appropriate disciplining of the child. She still feels uncomfortable about David's authority position over Joey, but she's also seeing positive results. Since Joey has a caring stepfather now, he is behaving better and is a happier and more secure child.

Some stepparents feel ineffectual about discipline because they want to be the perfect parent, whatever that might be! In their desire to please everyone, such timid persons allow the kids to walk all over their rights. And children of all ages are quick to take advantage of an uncertain adult. This problem arises with stepparents who have never before been parents. Anyone with the battle scars of parenthood knows that children will test your patience for as long as you allow bad behavior to continue. It is normal for adults to feel irritated by excessive noise, bickering, feet on furniture, nose picking, or whatever. Nonparents have the mistaken notion (perhaps acquired from TV or movies) that the good parent is all-understanding, is always absolutely fair, and has limitless tolerance for children's immature complaints. This fantasy parent is nonexistent.

Every household has a different set of rules for behav-

ior. What should you do if your stepchild is allowed to
throw clothes anywhere during visits with the real parent,
but you like all members of the family to hang up their
own things? "But Mom doesn't make me do it!" can be
handled with the statement that the rules are different
from home to home. In order to avoid confusion and
conflict, the new partners should sit down to define what is
acceptable behavior to them. The children know exactly
what is expected of them if the rules are made clear. Some
adults do not mind constant teasing, while others cannot
bear to hear older siblings tease their younger brothers or
sisters.

One eight-year-old boy was allowed to call his five-year-
old brother "Dumb-dumb." Every time he was addressed
as "Dumb-dumb," the younger boy started to cry. His new
stepmother would not allow this name-calling to continue.
The older boy was furious and ran to tell Dad how mean
his wicked-witch stepmother had been. The father told his
son that it was about time someone put a stop to his
cruelty. That settled the issue at his father's home. There's
no way the stepmother can change the boy's behavior
when he's with his real mother, and even an attempt would
be interpreted as an intrusion by his mother. But she does
have control in her own home.

Stepparent and mate should discuss deep disagreements
about discipline away from the children. Disagreements
on discipline frequently come across as uncertainty in the
eyes of the children, which in turn generates insecurity in
them. Besides, children love to hear fights between the
real parent and the intruding parent, particularly if the
kids themselves have manipulated the parents into the
fight. Children gain ammunition for upsetting the unsure
stepparent if they hear things like, "You can never lift a
hand to *my* child!" or, "Leave the kid alone—I'll handle
everything."

If you are a stepparent under discipline restrictions, you
must deal with the consequent feelings of frustration,

anger, and injustice. These feelings, if repressed, will eventually undermine your love relationship with your mate and warp any possibility of fully loving your inherited children. It is also unhealthy for the children to be disciplined only by the natural parent, as it teaches them how to turn parents against one another, allows them to poke fun at the powerless adult, and gives them an unnatural view of life, vis-a-vis adults. It is abnormal for the original parent to maintain control instead of sharing the discipline with his or her new mate. It is embarrassing and demeaning to the stepparent's view of himself. It just will not work. The importance of working out the rules of behavior, discipline, and rewards is that it gives the couple that much more emotional freedom to enjoy each other's company and to feed the original love a diet of affection and care.

One man who became a stepfather to three teenagers had to readjust his attitudes about free discussion. He had been reared in a patriarchal family in which the father sat at the head of the table, giving directions to his herd. No one would have dreamed or dared to contradict the father. He was addressed as "Sir." The mother deferred to her husband in all matters.

Although our new stepfather was contemporary enough in his attitudes to recognize that he had no wish to be a dictator, he was unprepared for his stepchildren's freedom of speech. Their mother was a brilliant person who was knowledgeable in many subjects. Her enjoyment of reading and discussing issues had been passed on to her son and daughters. Because the members of the family had such an intense interest in issues, they all loved to have heated discussions.

The rules for debate were that anyone had the right to voice an opinion about anything as long as that person was prepared to defend his or her position. This attitude was prevalent in daily conversations as well as in special rap sessions. After some months, the stepfather was able to see how this freedom of expression was a positive growth experience for the young adults. Their self-confidence was much higher than that of the average teenager. Today, the five of them can be seen arguing away with obvious enjoyment, and growing from the experience.

MONEY

Money matters can be disruptive in a marriage, and frequently are. Money is another important issue that is rarely discussed during courtship. Again, love without friendship does not allow couples to honestly state their views in a safe emotional atmosphere. What if you feel that children need an allowance, but your mate disagrees? Some people have a reward system for good grades. They tell their offspring that while they are young, their work in life is school and learning. If they work to their best capabilities, they get paid, just as in the outside world they will be paid well for good work. Other parents feel that children should not be paid for what they should do automatically. If you and your new mate talk about such matters in an objective light, some compromise can usually be reached.

CONSTANT COMPARING

The stepparent will have to accept the fact that the stepchildren will be comparing the stepparent with the real parent. Remember that children do not like divorce because it breaks up the whole family fantasy, even if that fantasy is completely unrealistic. If the natural parent lives far away, the child will invariably overidealize this absentee parent. The stepparent, already perceived as a stranger, will no doubt be negatively compared with the real parent. If you take children's viewpoints personally and if your self-confidence is low, such comparisons will certainly erode your self-esteem. It is normal for children to compare adults. It is also normal for stepchildren to vent their hostilities about the remarriage by making negative comparisons. The humorous approach by the stepparent will save him from feeling rejected.

Jody's stepchildren complained constantly about her "bad" cooking. There was always something wrong with whatever dish she prepared. It was too highly seasoned, too hot, too cold, or it just didn't taste like Mom's. Jody handled the grumbles by agreeing with them. She'd call them to meals with, "It's time for your awful dinner"; or, "I tried to make these hamburgers as bad as possible." Soon the kids were joking back and forth. They did not feel put down by Jody. She understood and accepted their need to compare her unfavorably with their Mom.

PROJECTED FEELINGS

Parents, stepparents, children, and stepchildren can suffer unnecessarily from projected feelings. The psychological defense mechanism of projection can best be understood by the following analogy. A film is a piece of celluloid with a picture imprinted on it. A projector transfers that picture onto a screen. Psychological projection is much the same. A person takes his or her feelings and projects them onto another individual. For example, a boy feels hateful, and he projects his hate onto the parents and thinks that they hate him.

Parents can also project their own fears and anxieties onto their children. A mother sent her little girl to kindergarten. The adult's own childhood had been traumatic, and she had been a fearful and insecure little girl. Her beginning school experience had been confusing and scarey. As a mother, she had been loving and successful. As a result, her own daughter was a happy little girl, eager to begin school.

On the third day of school, the woman went to pick up her daughter from the kindergarten room. The teacher said, "We had too many children in this room, so we transferred six of the brightest kids to the first-grade teacher." The mother felt immediate anxiety. She felt that this sudden shift would greatly upset her daughter.

She rushed to the first-grade room, eager to comfort her child. The daughter was happily coloring in a book, and when she saw her mother she said, "I passed into first grade in just three days! Isn't that nice?" The mother dropped her intention of speaking with the teacher. She had projected onto the current situation what her reaction would have been as a child; she would have been upset and confused by the change. Her daughter's reaction was just the opposite.

Another example of projecting feelings on children involves Don and his two boys, Joseph, six, and Craig, five. Don's stormy marriage ended when his wife walked out and left the state. Don was left with the two boys. Even though they didn't seem to miss her very much, Don was convinced they were in anguish. He stopped all discipline and let them do whatever they wanted.

Two boys of six and five can wreak havoc in a house, if permitted. They did just that. They stopped picking up their dirty clothes. While eating they scattered cereal all over the place and neglected to clean up their mess. They started to squabble and fight over every minor issue. They were allowed to become spoiled brats. No one could stand to be around them.

This situation went on for nearly three months. Don attributed their obnoxious behavior to their abandonment feelings. He kept saying, "The poor little guys have lost their mother." Actually, their behavior was the result of his lack of discipline. He was projecting his own feelings of despair and loss onto Craig and Joseph.

Don finally fell in love again, and his girl friend couldn't stand his children. She refused to come to Don's house unless he did something about the boys' wild antics. She also pointed out that the boys didn't seem to miss their mother at all. The force of her love brought Don back to his senses. He realized that he was projecting his feelings and that his behavior was actually harming his boys. Since children do not feel comfortable being out of control, Craig and Joseph soon responded to Don's reinstatement of rules and regulations.

The problem with projecting feelings is that most people are quite unaware that they are projecting. Someone else has to gently point out the phenomenon to the projecting person. As a new marriage partner you may see this phenomenon quite often. It will be your responsibility to point out this negative force to your husband or wife; it certainly is not healthy for either parent or child. Projecting also takes considerable emotional energy that should be invested positively in the marriage. Psychotherapy is sometimes the only way to break the projecting between parent and child.

ADULT STEPCHILDREN

Often a previously married man will marry a younger woman. She may even be close in age to his grown children. This situation makes it difficult for the younger woman to view herself as a stepparent to her husband's grown family. The young adults would only resent any of her attempts at mothering.

Try to become friends with your mate's adult children. If your mate has grown children who are close to your age and of the opposite sex, be prepared to handle a possible sexual attraction between the two of you. The normal barrier to emotional incest that exists between father and daughter, mother and son, is not present between stepparents and their inherited children. Remember that just because you are in love with a person does not mean you will never be attracted or attractive to other men or women.

If you sense a sexual attraction between yourself and one of your older stepchildren, admit it to yourself. Take steps to insure that you will not be put in a position that might encourage seductive behavior. Do not indulge in seminudity in front of teenagers. Discourage flirting or suggestive remarks. Do not feel guilty about sexual feelings, just take practical steps to avoid fanning the flame.

INTENSE PARENT-CHILD BONDING

The majority of stepparents we have talked with mention that, try as they might, they do not love their stepchildren with the same intensity as their natural children. This is to be expected. A profound and primitive parent-child bond is established even before birth. The pregnant woman begins to feel this bond when she first becomes aware of her pregnancy.

Primary bonding takes place interutero. The mother feels a primitive attachment to the fetus. This attachment may occur when she first discovers that she is pregnant or when she first feels the fetus moving within her. These close feelings grow during the pregnancy and reach a definite high when she first sees and holds the infant. Secondary bonding takes place at or after birth. The baby seeks to snuggle against the familiar smell and heartbeat of the mother. Her primitive instincts are to hold and care for the child she has carried.

The paternal bond, although much less intense, can also be felt by the expectant father. The father-child bond is qualitatively different than the mother's because of the obvious sexual differences. Frequently father bonding does not occur at all. Mother bonding fails to occur only when she is suffering from severe emotional illness.

Later, parents develop their love as the infant grows into childhood. Similarly, stepparents can develop love for their stepchildren. However, bonding and love are not the same thing. Bonding is a psychobiological phenomenon. Love is a psychological or emotional phenomenon. It is natural, then, for a stepparent to love his or her own children in a deeper way than the stepchildren, because the love for the natural child is supported by a strong natural bonding. The same principle holds true for children; their natural parents are usually loved more than the stepparent. Do not feel guilty, then, if you cannot lóve your stepchildren for some time. You have to give the relationship time to develop. If you never do develop that closeness with your stepchildren, don't try to force yourself. If it happens, it will do so naturally. The parenting you must give to your own children and to your stepchildren should be consistent and fair for all. Try to look at the family mix—yours, his or hers, and perhaps children of your new marriage—as "our gang."

UNREALISTIC WISHES

As a stepparent you may wish your inherited children to call you "Mom" or "Dad." They may not want to let you share that title with their original parents. Stepparents are usually called by their first name. It is unnecessary for the stepparent to feel rejected or belittled if the child opts for first names. After all, it is better than being called "Mr." or "Mrs.," or "Sir" or "Ma'am."

At times you may find yourself feeling self-pity for being used by a bunch of ungrateful beasts and misunderstood by your mate; in other words, generally prepared to drown the entire bunch. Remember during these natural low periods that parents with their own children experience these same feelings. Parenting ages adults, and the rewards of a job well done do not come until the child's own adulthood, if ever. Parenting is a job you have chosen. The rewards are minimal—another reason that mature adults should not live for their children. If they do, they may find they have lived for nothing, as any one child may return nothing. It makes far better sense to do the job of parenting simply for the sake of doing it, without feelings of sacrifice or anticipation of rewards. Do your job with the children the very best you can; but do not sacrifice your own potential happiness for it.

Chapter **9**

I Love You—I Hate You

AMBIVALENCE IS CONFUSING

Ambivalence—a psychological state in which one experiences simultaneous contradictory emotions toward a person—is present in most children in child-adult relationships, as well as in many parents. Ambivalent feelings are usually unresolved until the child becomes an adult. Even then some parents and their adult offspring respond to each other with a mixture of love and hate.

The normal ambivalence in biological families is mild when compared with the mixed feelings that a child has for a stepparent.

Ambivalence is a part of the human condition. It occurs in children because of the demands placed upon them by the parents. Children want to do what they desire, and do it "right now." This wish predominates because they are mostly self-centered during childhood. The parent, who desires age-appropriate behavior, becomes the frustrator of the child's selfish wishes. This frustration makes the child hate the parent. At the same time, the child loves and is dependent upon mother and father.

Parental ambivalence occurs because childcare is exhausting and, for the majority of time, unrewarding. Parents who grow up with the myth of the cherubic infant, happy-go-lucky toddler, and carefree teenager may experience great disappointment in their children's obnoxious behavior.

The daily stress of rearing children can, and frequently does, cause hateful feelings in parents. At the same time, parental love should be a constant most of the time. These confusing feelings can make a parent feel guilty because, after all, "We're 'supposed' to love our little ones all the time." Such love is as humanly impossible as it is for children to always love their parents.

Parents and children should all know that mixed feelings are a normal part of most relationships. It is a disservice to children's sense of reality if the parent expresses alarm over their offsprings' angry verbal expressions. If children say, "I don't like you" or "I hate you," they usually mean it only for the moment. They really are feeling the dislike or hatred. If you tell them, "You don't mean that" or "I'll never forgive you," you make them fearful and guilty about their anger. Hate is just as powerful an emotion as is love, and children should not be denied any of their feelings.

Parents often ask us, "What should I say when my child tells me he (she) hates me?" Our answer is to express whatever the parent is feeling, but to qualify the answer; for example, "I don't like you either, right now." Such responses seem quite acceptable to children. They give children an outlet for their frustration, let them know that the parents don't like them all the time, and put the situation in a time frame.

"REAL" VERSUS "STEP"

The ambivalence that stepchildren feel toward stepparents comes from the unconscious. The real parents are imprinted on the emotional tape in the unconscious. They are, to the child's unconscious, the real and only parents. Since this imprinted information is the child's unconscious view of normalcy, it rejects accepting a new and different parent. To the unconscious, then, there is only one set of parents. It is insignificant that the parents may have been deficient or even hated; they are still the "real" ones. This psychological factor is not designed to put down a step-parent; it simply exists and should be completely under-stood, so that the stepparent can objectively deal with it.

If you can grasp this important concept, your feelings need not be hurt when your stepchild suddenly blurts out, "You're not my real Mom (Dad)!" The child is reminding him- or herself of this fact as well as telling you. If you handle these situations with grace, in future years you will become the child's "real" friend long after he or she may have given up close feelings for the original parent.

To illustrate the power of the "one and only" set of parents: A patient, twenty-six, married, with two children of her own, had almost completed a successful analysis. Her father had died when she was twelve. In the course of treatment, resolving the problems that resulted from his death, she discovered that she had not liked him very much. She had, in fact, felt relieved at his death. Psycho-logically she buried her father and saw him in a realistic light, and emotionally she moved on.

Her relationship with her mother was mature and friendly. She was delighted when told that her mother, after fourteen years of widowhood, was going to remarry. The man was a warm and loving person, and the daughter truly liked him. All of these feelings were conscious; but, as we have discussed, the unconscious has views differing more widely from the conscious than most people are aware of.

The night before her mother's wedding, the patient had the following dream: She and her mother were sorting things from the past. Her mother picked up a tarnished silver tea set that had been a wedding gift from her first husband's parents. It was engraved with their names and the wedding date. Her mother said, "I won't need this anymore," and placed it to one side. The patient felt enraged in the dream and resented her mother's tossing away the gift.

When analyzed, her dream revealed that unconsciously she didn't want her mother to marry again. The tea set was symbolic of her original father and her parents' union. The mother was giving up the past and seeking happiness with a new man. The patient said that in the dream she felt as if her father were still alive and her mother were being disloyal to him. The new husband did not appear in the dream because to her unconscious he was not important. Keeping the mother loyal to the real father was the significant thing.

Because the patient was familiar with her unconscious, she easily accepted the dream as exposing her ambivalent feelings. She was amazed at her reaction to the happy event; however, it only validated again the rigid thinking of the "only parent" concept in the unconscious.

If a grown woman can experience this type of ambivalence, long past her dependency years, you can imagine a child's confusion when faced with love and hate feelings toward the intruding person.

Janice and Ted had been dating for several months. From experience, Janice did not include her children, Brenda, ten, and David, seven, in their plans. She had discovered since her divorce, two years before, that the children became too attached if she immediately introduced them to her current boy friend. They were always assuming that she would marry again and felt abandoned when a man stopped visiting. Janice wisely protected them and her dates from emotional involvement until she felt that a deep and lasting relationship was forming. The children had active lives and did not feel left out.

When Ted proposed, Janice accepted with delight. They

had both experienced a good deal of life and were mature and in love. They set the wedding date six months in the future so that Ted and the children could have a chance to get to know each other. He had met them, but very casually. His three children were either married or on their own, and had also met Janice under informal circumstances.

Gradually the new group became closer. Ted had an easy way with children, learned from his own family experiences, and the children responded to him. Since Brenda and David spent alternate weekends and vacations with their father, Janice and Ted had an opportunity to enjoy each other privately. This is one of the invisible benefits of an amicable divorce with liberal visitation rights. It periodically frees the parents from responsibility and gives them a breather. Janice and Ted took full advantage of their privacy and both looked forward to their marriage.

Their wedding was beautiful. They married in the summer and were able to take a luxurious two-week honeymoon, as the children were vacationing with their father. Although Brenda and David had been told of their mother's wedding plans, and had seemed happy about them, both children reacted with ambivalent feelings.

They had to relearn the daily sharing of their mother's attention. On the first night in the new household, when Janice and Ted were sitting together after dinner and David was ready for bed, he said good-by to Ted as he usually did. Ted reminded him that he lived there now, and David said, "But I thought you'd get married and just visit us!" As the days passed, Brenda took to interrupting Ted's every remark, showing quite a different attitude from the past, when she had been a busy young lady and not too interested in the adults' conversations.

Both children were experiencing the sudden shift of their positions in the new family. Because Ted understood their feelings, the transition from child-oriented home to normal family life was soon accomplished. He understood their ambivalent feelings and, by paying special attention, showed them how having another Dad around could be fun. He didn't take the ambivalent feelings personally.

FEELINGS OF DISLOYALTY

As most children respond positively to kindness and concern, stepchildren will eventually begin to like or love caring stepparents. At the same time, they must deal with their previous unconscious rejection of the "not real" parent. They must also handle their conscious feelings of being intruded upon by the new parent. Quite a load for a young person! Add this to all the other tasks of growing up, and it's no wonder that stepchildren at first seem confused toward the new parent.

Young children think that love is a quality that can be measured. They think that there is only so much of it. That is why a new baby on the scene is so threatening to their security. They think that if Mom and Dad love the new baby, they will take away five pounds of love for them. This immature thinking is doubly imposed upon stepparents.

In this connection, if children begin to feel love for a stepparent, they may often feel disloyal to the natural parent. They may fear that they can only love one mother or one father. Also, natural parents may feel jealous if their child loves a stepparent and may attempt to drive a wedge between the two. This jealousy is the result of low self-esteem. Unfortunately, this attitude restricts the child's autonomy and spontaneity by giving the child the message that love is to be given in measured lots.

If your stepdaughter seems to love you and then backs off, you can assume she is having problems with disloyal feelings toward her natural parent. You can easily teach her that it is possible and wonderful to love her real parents and you too. She may understand better if you use friends as an example. She probably has several friends whom she likes for different reasons. You can explain that everyone loves parents, friends, and grandparents in unique ways, and that the more people one loves, the bigger and better one becomes.

If you don't deal with your stepchildren's disloyal feelings, their guilt will cause them to provoke you to discipline them. Then they can "unlike" you and again feel loyal to the natural parent. Stepchildren have enough burdens and adjustments to make without having to deal with this problem too. The wise stepparent should be alert to children's symptoms of distress and pay attention to their need for being understood. You will be rewarded when the children enter adulthood and recall your helpful attention.

A teenager, with one foot planted in childhood and the other searching in midair, is a good example of ambivalence. He bounces from childhood's deep feelings of dependency to defiant adult independence. A part of him loves the parents, but the instinctual push to leave the nest makes him hateful and remote. The stepparent can easily become a target for the normal hostilities of the adolescent.

A classic example of a stepchild's ambivalence happened in our own family. Aaron, the father's son, had been talking one evening with his stepmother and gave a long account of his natural mother's wonderful cooking. Aaron's stepmother commented on his feelings of resentment toward her, as evidenced by this recital, and said that she understood them. Aaron was thirteen at the time and had been a stepchild for five years. He said that he frequently had a hard time because he and his stepmother got along so well, but that he would suddenly wish she weren't married to his father. Aaron was reassured that it was normal to experience these seesaw feelings; they talked at length about him, his mother and father, his stepmother's children, and his feelings about them.

It was a warm and honest discussion, which brought them closer together. When he kissed his stepmother good-night, he said, "I love you, Veryl, even though I sometimes wish you were dead." They both laughed at the seeming discrepancy of his statement, but Veryl felt validated as a mother that he could be so honest and secure with her. He felt accepted and comfortable.

Now that Aaron is in late adolescence, he no longer carries the wish for his old family. He has often thanked his stepmother for not getting angry or hurt when he talked about her as an outsider. They have a close and loving relationship, and when Veryl introduces him as her son, she feels it and so does he.

I LOVE YOU, BUT CAN'T TALK TO YOU

In some cases, the adolescent struggling for his identity may choose the natural parent as target and ignore the stepparent. The stepparent is not imprinted in the teenager's unconscious and is thus not the object of this rebellion. Here is an opportunity for the stepparent to act as a buffer between teenager and parent. Most normal adolescents usually feel misunderstood by and isolated from their parents. The stepparent may have a perfect opportunity to become the young person's advocate. However, the teenager must be aware that the stepparent's loyalty is to the natural parent.

In a recent national survey by a family magazine, the majority of teenagers responding stated that they loved their parents. They also reported that they could not talk about their feelings with their parents. This response was not surprising to us, as we have found out that most adults do not know how to talk with each other about intimate worries, let alone with a hostile teenager.

Getting adolescents to reveal their feelings is not an easy task. The stepparent who wishes to ease the ambivalent atmosphere between parent and teenager can learn the art of eliciting open talk. If you put forth the effort to become a friend to a confused adolescent stepchild, he or she will be *your* friend in adulthood.

Adolescents are uncomfortable sitting down and talking face-to-face, simply because eye contact is embarrassing for them. They still have the childhood notion that adults can read their minds. They also think that adults can see in their eyes the sexual fantasies they are having. The guilty feelings cause them to feel nervous and thus to avert their eyes.

In order to put a teenager at ease, provide for a setting that is as casual as possible. The most relaxed atmosphere can be obtained by arranging for some mutual physical activity. When you are working together, a sense of camaraderie begins to grow.

Since teenagers are by nature suspicious of adults, you can lessen their paranoia by talking about yourself first. If you expose your remembered adolescent insecurities, you will signal that everyone has a hard time growing up. Most teenagers feel that they are the *only* person who ever suffered from poor body image, anxieties about the opposite sex, guilt over masturbation and sexual fantasies, enormous appetites, love and hate for parents and siblings, fear of peer rejection, and occasional homosexual thoughts.

The discovery that all teenagers, past and present, have similar anxieties lifts a tremendous burden from the usual adolescent. Because of the boys-against-the-girls programing during childhood, the teenager is usually amazed to be told that most males and females suffer similar worries. The friend-stepparent can thus pass on information and answer questions that the stepchild may feel unable to ask a natural parent.

The teenage person today has a much more difficult future than the young person of just ten or fifteen years ago. Today's youth have fewer job possibilities and no guarantees. They cannot even count on automatic employment if they attend college. The unstructured social scene gives teenagers no model for expected behavior. The heroes of just a few years ago are gone, or maybe even in jail. Sympathy for the plight of young adults is appropriate, for the world they are about to enter is a very unstable one.

A stepparent may be able to offer this empathetic attention better than a parent. Talking intimately about reality draws people closer together. Teenagers are trying to pull away from the natural parents and shy away from exposing themselves to them. The stepparent is a natural outlet.

Whenever an adolescent does talk to you with openness and trust, reassure him or her that the conversation will be confidential, and make sure that it is. Fear of ridicule and lack of respect for their privacy keeps many young people mute around adults. You can always correct their fears by being a true and loyal confidant.

THE GROWN CHILD DEPARTS

The parenting role is just a part of marriage. Even though it sometimes seems to consume a very large part of your life, parenting must be placed in perspective. The children do eventually leave home and begin their separate lives. Hopefully this separation can be a happy occasion for everyone. Ambivalent feelings may erupt when the parent experiences both relief to see the young adult leave and a desire to keep the maturing offspring under the protective wing of the family.

These feelings should be ventilated between the parenting adults. Usually, relief becomes the dominant feeling as parents become a couple again with all the freedom and privacy they never experienced while the children were in the home. For stepparents, it will be the first time they have had the partner exclusively to themselves. We are sure you will discover how wonderful that privacy can be. It's time for the second honeymoon. This one should be better than the first, in that this one is really earned.

Sometimes, at the point when the offspring are on the threshold of independence, children's and parents' ambivalence is so great that nothing can be done to dissolve it. It seems that all is hopeless, but the adults do have an option. Consider the choice made by Jody, daughter of Lucille.

Lucille and Allan brought to their marriage a mixture of children. Lucille had two daughters, Adele, eighteen, and Jody, sixteen, and a ten-year-old son, John. Allan had custody of his son, Joey, age nine. The younger boys quickly became friends. Adele was home only as a visitor on vacations from college. Jody, still in high school, was a misfit. She felt left out, imposed upon, and jealous. Coupled with all the usual turmoil of her age, her feelings became too much to handle.

Lucille's and Allan's efforts to help her were unsuccessful. They tried talking, but she became more withdrawn and sullen. Jody's jealousy showed in her constant picking on the younger boys. At the same time, she seemed to like Allan, but only showed her affection when no one else was around. Prior to her mother's remarriage, she had displayed none of these obnoxious traits. It was obvious, therefore, that her responses were stimulated by the new home situation.

After six months of Jody's disruptive behavior, Lucille and Allan gave her a choice. She could try to understand herself and them by talking it out, see a therapist for adolescents, go to boarding school, or live elsewhere. By giving Jody a list of options, this couple sent her the message: "You can't indulge your anger on four other people any longer." Lucille and Allan did not feel guilty or heartless. They had chosen each other and were trying to live a loving life. They had tried to help Jody with all their resources and were rebuffed.

Jody was relieved, as she hated herself for her reaction to the entire family. She chose to live with an aunt who was willing to have her. Her departure was cool but not hysterical. Because Lucille and Allan felt justified and relaxed about their decision, they were able to be objective. They did not accuse or reject Jody, and she was told she could come back any time.

Her aunt was a pleasant woman who handled the whole

thing as a positive experience. In the months that followed Jody regained the sense of self that she had lost when "all those people moved in on me." She liked living with her aunt's smaller family. And Lucille and Allan knew that unnecessary suffering is a waste of valuable living time. There are solutions to any problems that arise in life. Since they are created by humans, they can be solved by them.

As with all other problems of stepparenting, if ambivalence can be understood as a normal reaction of children, it loses its power to disrupt your equilibrium. Because the nuclear family has the emotional umbrella provided by their physical bond, natural parents are better able to take these love-hate feelings than stepparents. But the adult can, by empathizing with the new stepchild, gradually lead him or her out of the limbo of ambivalence. Admittedly, doing this takes a tough skin, objectivity, and a large dose of humor. The rewards of returned love, however, are worth every effort.

Chapter **10**

The Absent Parent

IDEALIZING THE LOST PARENT

Charles was a stepfather for Jeremy, age seven, and Lindy, age four. Charles had never been a biological father, but he always liked kids. He had been a camp counselor during his adolescence and enjoyed the work. He was an avid outdoorsman and assumed that his stepchildren would share his enthusiasm. Although Sheri, his new wife, had always been a city girl, she was willing to try new experiences.

Charles, naturally a happy-go-lucky man, found himself becoming increasingly irritated in the course of the first camping trip with his new family. Every time Charles tried to teach Jeremy a new skill, he was met with a put-down: "My Dad could put a tent up a lot faster than that"; "My Dad would have twenty-nine fish by now"; "You should see how my Dad can get a fire going." Little Lindy would echo her brother's remarks in "me too" fashion.

When the children were asleep and Sheri and Charles sat by the campfire, he said he was beginning to feel inferior. "That first husband of yours must have been quite a guy," was Charles' comment. Sheri started to giggle and finally said, "That first husband couldn't even bait a line. He never took the kids around the block, let alone into the woods. And, since he's been gone for two years, the kids can hardly remember him. Just relax, Charley— they're just reminding themselves that they once had a Dad."

This fantasizing and making up an ideal past with an absent parent is one of the "switch" ways children may deal with loss. Jeremy and Lindy were too young to understand or cope with the knowledge that their Dad was an uncaring and unloving man. He never attempted to visit them and refused to pay child support.

Little children cannot imagine that a parent does not love them. They attempt to master the loss by idealizing the lost parent. Since children have vivid imaginations, they give the absent parent superhuman powers.

This idealization of the lost parent can be quite difficult for a stepparent to handle. If you remember, however, that a child is dealing with loss and not trying to put you down, the idealization need not be taken personally. It is normal for a stepparent to feel that the child is being ungrateful. The reality is that no child is grateful for any parenting. A child takes it for granted. Children have no concept of their parents' hard work, of their struggles with budgeting time and money, or of their financial sacrifice.

When young children idealize a lost parent, the best way to handle their fantasies is to ignore the grandiose statements. It is dangerous to put down a previous parent. The children will learn the truth themselves later on. The majority of stepparents we have spoken with feel defensive when a stepchild elaborates all the good qualities of an adult who is known to be rotten or offensive. They want to tell the child the truth and defend their role of taking on someone else's responsibilities.

This attitude only backfires on the stepparent. Children live more in the imagination than in reality. Brusquely taking away their fantasy image of a lost parent leaves them floundering. It robs them of their tool for dealing with their feelings of abandonment. An adult can cope with life problems with reason and logic, mature mechanisms that children have not yet developed. They'll develop them, usually during adolescence.

If a stepparent wisely allows children their fantasies, in time the youngsters will replace idealization with reality. In fantasizing, they are self-protectively denying the fact that Mom or Dad doesn't care about them. Slowly they will absorb the information that the stepparent, and not the real and lost parent, is the adult who cares for their needs. This insight takes time, and therefore patience is required from the stepparent. No day-to-day parent can match up to a dream parent; so don't expect to, and your feelings won't be hurt. Equate the child's idealizations with hero-worship of a television star. A part of the child, but only a minute part, knows that the feats of strength he or she sees in the mind's eye are fictional.

One young stepfather related the following story to our group of stepparents. His four young stepchildren tried to intimidate him every time he disciplined them. "Just you wait till Daddy gets here"; "Boy, oh boy, will Daddy ever beat you up"; and other dire threats were made. At the same time, the brood enjoyed the positive attention given to them by their stepfather. Unlike their real father, he helped them with their homework, listened to their problems with their friends, and encouraged them to be individuals.

When "Daddy" did arrive for his brief annual visit, the stepfather was quite amused; for the giant of the children's imaginations was a slight, nonthreatening, and depressed man who obviously could not beat up anyone. In the children's eyes, however, he was virile and strong. Of course, they forgot their promise of Daddy's revenge, not because they were suddenly faced with reality, but because they were more happy to visit with their father than to seek revenge on their stepfather.

By not responding to his stepchildren's fantasy threats,

this stepfather gave the children emotional room to discharge normal ambivalent feelings and to experience the wish, also normal, that the original family would regroup. The children eventually dropped their empty threats, as they saw that their stepfather had no desire to interfere with their relationship with their natural father.

If the absent parent is actually cruel and uncaring, the children will eventually find out for themselves. And they must be allowed to see reality, accept the situation, talk about their disappointments, and eventually see the idealized parent in a realistic light.

Marnie sought help in adjusting to her second marriage. While discussing her husband's reaction to her children, she related that when their natural father called the children, he made them many promises. Marnie said her heart went out to her children as their faces lit up with anticipation. The father, an alcoholic, always called the children when he was in a drunken, blabbering mood. He sounded like a tipsy Santa Claus, promising them trips to Disneyland, outrageous presents, and a visit "in a few days." These promises would then be related to Marnie and their stepfather. Marnie's husband made the mistake of telling the children that all of their Dad's exaggerated promises were not going to come true. Of course, Dad didn't arrive in a few days, nor did any of the trips or presents ever materialize.

Because children are without logic, Marnie's offspring drew the conclusion that their stepfather was responsible for the father's nonappearance and breaking of promises. After all, the stepfather had *said* it wouldn't happen. Since it didn't, he must, therefore, be the cause of their disappointment. If the stepfather had let the children find out for themselves that the real father was undependable, the children's anger and disappointment would have been directed to the appropriate person.

Marnie's husband, with all good intentions, was trying to protect the children by warning them. They, however, did not understand this reality approach. They just thought he was keeping their father away. Trying to protect children from truth does not always work. The next time father called with his inflated plans, Marnie and her husband made no comment. When the children had to deal with the disappointment of no visit, they knew whom to blame.

Their mother and stepfather were able to help at this point by explaining to the children just what happens when a person drinks too much. They said that people feel generous and make wild promises, but that they really can't follow through. They helped the children begin to understand that their father's drinking was not caused by them. It was his own problem, unrelated to the children's needs.

Further calls from their father were treated lightly by the children, with no expectations on their part. Marnie and her husband allowed the children to experience disappointment and anger. But they were also available to the children to buffer their hurt and to explain the father's unusual behavior.

None of us can protect our children from everything painful in life. To do so would be unfair to them, as it would send them into the world without emotional resources to deal with pain, disappointment, and rejections, of which they will receive plenty. Children must learn that life is not always fair and consistent. They must also learn from experience that many adults act like children. Some of those adults just might happen to be their own parents.

MISPLACED RAGE

One young man hated his stepmother with such intensity that he was referred for treatment. In reality, his stepmother was a nice person, and a responsible mother to her own children. She was pleasant and welcoming to her three stepchildren whenever they visited. Everyone was alarmed by the hostility and hate of Mark, age fifteen, toward his stepmother. He refused to talk to her when she asked him anything. When his father took Mark aside to find out why Mark was so hateful, the boy could not explain.

In treatment he revealed that he hated his father's new wife because she was responsible for his horrid plight in life. His real mother began to drink heavily after her ex-husband, Mark's father, remarried. She had been all right during the first two years since her divorce; but she was infuriated when her ex married after that period of time.

When Mark would be sound asleep, his mother would stumble into his room, awaken him, and begin to cry. She would bitterly complain about how his father's new wife had ruined her life, making her drink too much. Mark knew this was crazy, drunken talk, but he began to hate his stepmother just the same. His mother would go out at night and drink in bars. She would call home, wake up Mark, and demand that he come and get her. The mother's alcoholism was a terrible burden for the fifteen-year-old. He was made to feel responsible for his mother's safety. She was so filled with self-pity that he couldn't let her see how angry she made him. He was afraid to tell his father what was going on at home. Thus, he turned his rage toward his stepmother.

Since the mother was the person in emotional turmoil, it was suggested indirectly that she seek professional help. Her infantile behavior was disrupting two families, and, in particular, a young, shaky teenager. During his mother's recovery, Mark moved to his father's home. Relieved of his enforced responsibilities, he soon began to respond to his stepmother's sympathetic warmth.

FAIRYTALE VISITS

Sometimes a child will idealize an absent parent with encouragement from that parent. When divorced, many parents move far away from their children and are able to visit only once a year, at most. When the visiting parent arrives, the child and that parent usually strive for a perfect time together. For most children, a perfect time means getting their own way. A visiting parent, perhaps out of guilt or out of anxiety to please a semiabandoned child, will try to show the child a perfect time. The parent will leave the day's itinerary open to the child's choice and whim. Movies, restaurants, and toy shops are at the child's disposal, along with the parent's undivided attention.

Few families have the financial security or the desire to indulge a child's every wish. Anyway, such indulgence would be detrimental to the child's maturing process. But as children are self-centered, they think that getting all those goodies would be just fine.

Since the visits are so infrequent, the child will try to please the parent, and often will avoid any confrontation and will repress any angry feelings such as: "Why did you leave me in the first place" "How come you don't visit more often?" or, "When can I come and live with you?" The whole setup manages to avoid any guilt on the parent's part or anger on the child's part. It is an unconscious pact to have a vacationlike atmosphere and avoid real problems. The parent then leaves. The child abruptly returns to the reality of life—one natural parent and one stepparent.

Home, after an ideal vacation visit, can look pretty grim. There are no choices of menu as in restaurants, and one may even have to help clear and do the dishes. The emotional shift is quite severe for a child. Expect your youngster to be irritable for a day or two after one of these fantasy trips has come true. The child should also be encouraged to talk about his or her negative feelings. The wise at-home parent and stepparent must get the message across that no one lives so grandiosely in a daily family situation. Whether or not the child actually believes you will depend on his or her age. Be careful not to put down the careless, overly generous parent.

If possible—and we understand it is not always possible

—the father or mother should talk to the visiting, idealized parent and ex-mate and ask that person to ease up on the Disneyland approach. If the visiting parent can grasp the difficulties of adjustment after a fairytale visit, he or she might accept your suggestion.

If your spouse is unable to sanely discuss issues with his or her ex-mate, then you usually won't be any more successful. Patiently, you'll have to reveal to the child that life's constants are what bring a secure sense of family love. You, not the absent natural parent, will be the one present when the school calls a PTA conference, when a knee needs a bandage, when a nightmare causes screams in the dark, and also when there are good times to be shared.

You can reveal, by word and action, that you understand how the child might be angry at all the parents in his or her life, including you.

As children grow older, they will grow bored with the game of having their love bought. They will also notice that their at-home parent is a happier person in the second marriage. With this realization, a lessening of the idealization of the absent parent begins.

FANTASIZING

Some parents actually lay a fantasy trip on their children. This usually occurs when a man or woman loses a mate because of a love affair. The partner who is left single feels humiliated and inferior. These initial feelings are appropriate if someone enters and replaces one's position. In reality, those marriages that are broken over love affairs were probably not very satisfactory to begin with. It is rare for happily married people to risk spoiling a marriage by having affairs; and if they do take the risk, they manage not to get caught, as there is too much to lose.

Beverly's husband, Dick, left her, after seven years of frustration, for another woman. Dick had met Ann and gradually, over a year's period, he fell in love with her. He received so little emotional support, affection, or sexual gratification from Beverly, that it was easy for him to respond to Ann's natural giving nature.

As we have discussed before, the unconscious seeks to repeat a person's past experiences. Beverly's coldness was the same as that of Dick's mother. He had entered psychoanalysis after five years of unhappiness with Beverly. During the analysis, he discovered that he had unconsciously chosen a mate with his mother's qualities. He tried to get his wife to enter treatment, but she refused—a tragic decision, as analysis can help a person change from an ungiving one to a loving one.

After the divorce, Beverly began to idealize her past marriage. Her idealization was an attempt to deny blame or responsibility for any failure on her part. She told friends, acquaintances, and her four-year-old daughter that Dick and she had been extremely happy until Ann came and "stole his heart."

Because no one knows the intimate details of another's marriage, people believed Beverly's tale of woe. Her daughter naturally also believed her and hated Ann. Beverly actually kept her fantasy active for five more years, managing to drive a wedge between Dick and his daughter. He was not able to repair that damage until his daughter became a young adult and could understand the value and beauty of being in love. By denying her faults, Beverly wasted her life, cast a negative image on Ann, withheld her daughter's love from her father—and lost everybody in the end.

If you are the victim of such a fantasizing adult and are labeled a seducer or seductress, do not be defensive. Other people's gossip will quickly fade. They will become bored with the first mate's endless idealizing of the old, long-dead marriage. Time will reveal to all that you and your mate are actually happy. If you can, try to empathize with the losing partner, knowing that the fantasy marriage is an attempt to shore up sagging self-esteem.

Many stepparents ask us, "What about *my* self-esteem?

I'm trying to make a marriage work under very stressful conditions. I have five kids to deal with, all with traumatic backgrounds; I have to run a household, hold down a job, and maintain myself."

Our answer is that self-esteem comes from personal accomplishments plus personal relationships. A person's sense of worth should be nourished every day. The small accomplishments, such as accepting a stepchild's first acknowledgment of you as a good person, receiving the smile of a husband or wife for your help, becoming more organized, doing a good job at work, giving love and affection to your family, all should boost your self-esteem.

Rod Steiger, one of America's most gifted actors, made a most eloquent statement about personal self-esteem. In an interview by *People* magazine about his performance in "W. C. Fields and Me," he was asked to comment on his success. He stated that to him there was no such thing as success, only "renewed arrival." As psychoanalysts, we are in complete agreement with Mr. Steiger. Every day is an opportunity for renewed arrival in our quest for personal growth and happiness.

With the emotional overload that comes with the job of stepparenting, one's goals should definitely be directed toward renewed arrival rather than instant success.

Chapter **11**

Dealing with Strong Feelings

NEGATIVE FEELINGS MAY SURFACE

Just as it takes time for stepchildren to accept a new parent, it will also take you, as stepparent, time to adjust to your new family. You will not immediately feel comfortable when you join an established family. You will have to deal with feelings of rejection, jealousy, and anger. Everyone wishes to be liked, and it hurts deeply when stepchildren seem intent on hating the new parent.

Recently, during a group discussion with some stepparents, one woman stated that her biggest hurdle with her stepson was that he reminded her that her husband had a previous sexual relationship. She candidly admitted that she didn't want her husband ever to have been in love with anyone but herself. The boy was constant proof that her mate had loved, or at least had had intercourse with someone before her. She stated that it didn't matter to her that her husband's first marriage had been unfulfilling. She was quite aware that her feelings were irrational. Intelligence plays little role when it comes to feelings, and especially to jealousy. She said that during the first six months of their marriage she had a difficult time even looking at the boy. Her feelings were a mixture of jealousy of the past and revulsion toward the need for childcare.

How did she resolve her unhealthy attitude? First, she realized that she was becoming more absorbed in her negative feelings than in her positive love for her husband. Second, although with great embarrassment, she discussed her feelings with her husband. Much to their surprise, they discovered that they had mutual feelings, for he admitted that he was experiencing the same jealousy about her past. He was a stepfather to her two daughters, so it was obvious that she had made out at least a couple of times.

This couple, by hiding their "irrational" feelings from each other, were needlessly using up emotional energy, energy that belonged in their present love and marriage and not in the past. After they talked openly, the negative feelings subsided. They were able to see the humor in their feelings. The jealousy of the past and the wish for exclusive possession comes from the selfish, irrational part of one's nature that wants everything. This couple used their rational minds to reason that the past was a fact of life and irreversible. Disclosing their selfish wishes for possession by verbalizing them helped to alleviate the jealousy and free more energy for loving.

Many stepparents feel guilty about their seemingly senseless feelings of jealousy and rejection. They feel foolish to be envious of their mate's love for the offspring. The guilt then erodes their self-esteem and compounds feelings of rejection. We hope it will be helpful to these stepparents to know that this jealousy is quite normal and is felt by every new stepparent at one time or another.

The feelings, however, must be discussed. If left unexpressed, jealousy and rejection can turn into depression or become disguised in psychosomatic illness. If you as a stepparent feel that your mate would become defensive or alarmed by your feelings, then talk to another stepparent or a nonjudgmental friend. If these outlets are unavailable, by all means seek professional help.

A THERAPIST CAN HELP

A competent, experienced therapist will have heard your story many times and will not put you down for your "bad" feelings. Usually when people seek psychotherapy they feel helpless because of an inability to solve their own problems. Such helplessness is particularly true in men, who have been programed to be strong in all situations. Feeling helpless makes a person feel childlike. This regressed state of mind can interfere with sound judgment when looking for a therapist. One may tend to assume everything the therapist says is correct just because he or she is a professional.

One cannot tell if a therapist is competent by the number of diplomas hanging on the office wall, for psychotherapy and counseling are arts. Some therapists are very gifted in their art; and some, no matter how many years of training they may have had, are not gifted at all. If and when you seek a therapist, inquire of friends who may be under treatment. If they have improved their emotional state, the therapists they recommend are most likely competent. A trusted physician might be a good referral source for you, although professional loyalty frequently fogs judgment.

Whomever you make an appointment with, remember that you do have a choice of therapists, even if you are plagued with feelings of helplessness. If you don't like the therapist, go to someone else. You will want to work with someone who makes you feel comfortable. If a therapist starts recommending pills as a solution to your problems, you're in the wrong place. Pills only cover up symptoms and are not curative. You've already got one serious problem. You don't need to become an addict in addition. Emotional upheavals have no magical solutions. Talking with an objective and understanding professional person is curative.

As a prospective client you have the right to ask any therapist about his or her life attitudes. If your number-one life priority is to have loving relationships, you will want to know if your therapist shares that priority. If you are going to trust your therapist, you have to know something about him or her. Gone are the days, as they should be, of instant respect for professionals. Medical therapists and professors who are therapists, in particulr, seem to enjoy being all-powerful. Remember, *M.D.* does not stand for *Minor Deity.* Again, a referral by someone you know who has had a similar past problem and has been helped is the very best one. Never blindly call a mental-health clinic or a name from the Yellow Pages.

GUIDELINES FOR COMMUNICATING

The ideal situation, of course, would be open discussions between spouses who could talk to each other without becoming threatened by intense feelings. Such openness is possible when, as we stated before, friendship is the foundation for the marriage.* Since talking about angry or hurt feelings is very difficult for most people, we offer some guidelines on the art of communicating. These rules must have mutual acceptance by couples or they will not work.

FIND AN APPROPRIATE TIME AND PLACE TO TALK ABOUT FEELINGS. It is self-defeating to try to start an emotionally charged conversation just before going to work, just after arriving home from work, or in the midst of dinner. You should absolutely never try it if one of you is drunk.

Since both of you will be attempting a new form of open communication, you will want an atmosphere conducive to

*See Part I, Chapter 3, pages 37-39.

talking. Try to find a nondistracting place. Make arrangements for the children to be involved in their own activities. Turn the TV set off and forget about answering the phone.

If you cannot find privacy in your own home (even in the bedroom), then change the scene. Two people we know do their intimate talking in a restaurant. Another couple may find a motel room a neutral place for discussing unpleasant feelings. Use your imagination, and the two of you will find an appropriate time and place.

If you cannot comply with the first rule, then one or both of you are unconsciously trying to sabotage growth. If this is so, you will have to question what your fears are about revealing your feelings.

Many people have been reared in environments that precluded even acknowledging feelings. Their unconscious sends them messages that talking about irrational feelings will only bring displeasure and rejection. They then overcome this unconscious fear by never having enough time to get down to gut issues. This evasion is just a cover-up for rejection fears and must be overcome in order to move on. If each person promises beforehand not to reject the other, the entire experience can be a corrective one. It will refute the unconscious fear that openness brings rejection.

REALIZE THAT ANGER IS PERMISSIBLE. Angry feelings are a normal result of frustration, misunderstanding, and feeling unloved. Neither person should be put down for expressing anger, even if the outburst gets intense and loud. Each has the right to be listened to without the other person putting up defenses, counterattacking, or falling apart.

VERBALIZE YOUR ANGER. It is far more productive to say, "I'm mad and this is why," than to clam up, pout, or become tearful.

BE RESPONSIBLE FOR DEFINING YOUR WORDS.
This rule is especially important. "You know what I mean"
is lazy language, and requires the other person to read
minds. As we grow up, we all attach significant feelings to
certain words. When you say "love," "fear," "hurt," "joy,"
"need," or any other word connected with emotions, explain to your partner what that word means to you. By
taking the time and energy to explore and define your
own meanings, you can avoid the frustration of being
misunderstood.

BE KIND. After all, the reason for any intimate talking
is to grow closer to each other by resolving conflicts together. Kindness means trying to empathize with your
mate's feelings. This empathy is achieved by attempting to
put yourself in the other's emotional shoes. Try objectively
to see yourself and your actions as your mate is experiencing you.
   This form of kindness also involves the ability to admit
your own imperfections. It is so easy to see another's
faults, but we all are very accepting of our own foibles.
Remember that a critical remark about one facet of your
personality does not negate your entire self. If you let
yourself feel rejected after one critical remark, you can
lose sight of your goal of growing up and becoming closer.

LAUGH AT YOUR MISTAKES. Laughing at your shortcomings is a simple matter if you can accept the fact that
you are not that illusive perfect person. Laughing about
your own faults increases your self-esteem and has the
effect of clearing the air. Your mate may then also assume
this perspective.

DON'T INTERRUPT. This rule is the most difficult,
though simple. Your turn will come. Interrupting while
the other person is talking is disrespectful of that person's
feelings. It may also be based on the fear that you will not

have your chance to speak up. Such thoughts will not occur if both of you have entered into the discussion with a fair attitude.

HAVE RESPECT FOR EACH OTHER'S PRIVACY. Make a pact not to reveal to outsiders your partner's secrets of the heart. This promise will only increase your love and friendship.

Any skill takes time to learn. If the two of you stick to the guidelines, you will learn to feel more connected with each other. This foundation of sharing leads to more frank talks about anxieties and fears we must all resolve. Confiding our innermost selves to an accepting, loving partner eases the sense of aloneness everyone experiences.

When you both have learned this art, you can then teach your children how to express themselves openly. This is particularly important for children who have traveled the painful road of family breakup and their parents' re-marriages.

RESENTMENTS ARE NORMAL

Many stepparents feel resentful toward their mate's first partner because of the damage they may have done to the children's personalities.

Erin fell in love with Dick. They had both been previously married. Erin had no children, but Dick was custodial parent of his son, Jamey, age three. Jamey's mother had emotionally and physically abandoned the boy since birth. When Erin met the child, he was totally unmanageable. He still drank from a bottle, was not toilet trained, and could not speak beyond a shrill whine. He had been psychologically tested and was declared mentally retarded.

Erin came from a stable family with little trauma in her childhood. She figured she could save this little boy. And she did. She decided to toilet train him, and accomplished that task in two weeks. She began talking, singing, and reading to him. He began to achieve higher than normal verbal skills within six months. He developed regular eating and drinking habits. Mentally retarded? Not at all. He needed love and Erin gave it to him. He was tested again at the age of six and found to be of highly superior intelligence.

He retained one psychological defect that Erin could not overcome. That defect was a constant anxiety that vibrated from his little being. He could rarely sit still, was a constant chatterer, and had to eat enormous amounts of food (lunch could easily consist of seven hot dogs with buns, a can of beans, and three or four doughnuts). This kind of anxiety is called *abandonment anxiety*, and results from severe early maternal deprivation.

Erin had deep and appropriate resentment toward Jamey's biological mother. She could not imagine how a mother could reject an infant and watch him deteriorate. Erin's resentment only increased when, after an absence of four years, the mother reappeared and wanted to visit with Jamey. The court allowed the visits, but Jamey did not allow his real mother into his heart. His psychological mother was Erin. Being such a bright little boy, he learned to become so obnoxious and unmanageable with his real mother that she soon stopped her visits.

He's ten now, and the abandonment anxiety has eased a great deal. This stepmother saved a life. Her resentments found an outlet in talking about her feelings with her supportive husband, but they still linger. No one really enjoys taking care of another person's indulgent mistakes. By admitting that it's no fun and that one has fantasies of destroying the neglectful first parent, and by talking openly to a nonjudgmental person about any such wishes, a stepparent can avoid an ulcer herself and help the stepchild grow into a healthier child.

What to do if no one seems to appreciate your efforts? No matter how generous child-support payments may be, they never seem to cover everything. Stepfather, probably paying for his first family too, has the additional financial burden of his second family. Meanwhile, the stepchildren are giving him the usual hassles of natural growth phases, plus normal resentments of his presence. What man wouldn't feel resentful?

Children do not understand or care about the stresses that adults undergo in making a living, driving on the expressway, fighting through crowds, or dealing with the business world. They don't care, as they are in a normal state of self-absorption. All parents will feel the ingratitude of their children over the usual sacrifices made for them. An understanding mate, to whom one can gripe, is helpful when a stepparent is feeling resentful.

This ability or opportunity to complain in an accepting atmosphere is necessary. We all need an outlet for our frustrations, and the best place for it is in the home.

What can you do when the in-laws delight (intentionally or not) in talking about the ex as if he or she were the most delightful person that ever lived? This encourages the children to agree, with looks of glee or revenge thrown in the direction of the stepparent. This situation is unfair. It is up to the husband or wife whose parents are behaving this way to put a stop to it. After all, people who love each other should also protect each other from outside hostilities.

THE NEW BABY ARRIVES

If the new couple have a child of their own, the stepparent may also have to deal with the anger of in-laws, the ex, and the stepchildren. It is perfectly reasonable for a loving couple to want to celebrate that love by having a baby. It is better if they don't, but understandable if they do. However, it will be acceptable *only* to the new couple.

The new baby's stepbrothers and stepsisters will not like the new arrival at all, for the arriving infant will be a symbol that this new marriage is for real. The newborn's half-siblings will be jealous because the new child will spend the whole time with "real" parents. Stepchildren who visit never feel that they get their full share of the parents' attention. And they don't.

The ex and the in-laws on both sides will have to face reality also. If one's ex actually starts a new family, the fantasy of getting back together is dashed. The initial anger of one's own children from a previous marriage and of one's stepchildren can be handled if they are all allowed to discharge such feelings verbally. Again, the parent must put aside all alarm about the intense feelings children may have.

Sibling rivalry is normal. No child wants to be displaced by another, but correct parental attitude will help the child deal with jealousy. Stepchildren who must accept a baby into the new family need a lot of support from both parents.

We have found that storytelling helps a youngster who is unable to speak directly about fears of rejection and anger. One three-year-old told her pregnant stepmother the following gruesome tale in response to the question, "Tell me how you feel about babies":

"Once upon a time there was a little girl named Maryanne. Not me, Maryanne, but another girl. She was really mad at her parents. She dug a big hole and made a big fence around it . Then she pushed her Dad and Aunt Sue [her name for stepmother] into the hole. She threw in the baby too. Then she threw in fire, and when they yelled for her to let them out, she wouldn't let them."

This story was related with great glee and sparkling eyes. If the stepmother had reacted to the little girl with alarm, her angry feelings would have been suppressed and would eventually surface elsewhere. Her stepmother, Aunt Sue, just said, "She must really have been mad." "Yes," said Maryanne, "but scared too." "If you ever feel that angry or scared, come to Daddy and me, and we'll hug you till you feel better." "Okay," said Maryanne and, relieved of her feelings, skipped off to play.

The small child was unaware that she had relieved her negative feelings toward the new baby because she was given room to tell her "story." The parent knew, though, and that's the main point. Allowing a verbal outlet in the context of "just a story" gives the child a verbal arena for anger.

CHILD ABUSE

We must inject a subject here that most people would rather ignore—child abuse. We define *child abuse* as the actions the adult takes when he or she cannot control feelings of rage or disappointment with an infant or child and physically or psychologically batters the child's body or ego. Abuse can take the physical forms of whipping; breaking bones by punching or kicking; burning fingers and feet; tying up children; sequestering children in closets for days, months, or years; throwing children through windows; and sexually assaulting children—to name a few.

The psychological child abuser neglects the child's need for love and approval. Such neglect can occur by ignoring the child's existence, constantly calling him derogatory names, and eroding his self-esteem through sarcasm.

Parents and stepparents can be child abusers. The incidences of child battering run through every social and economic level of our society. Parents who abuse a child often feel justified in their cruelty. They most probably were abused themselves during childhood. The unconscious then considers child beating or molesting as normal.

The child abuser often expects much more from the infant or child than is humanly possible. Babies do not cry for prolonged periods because they *want* to upset adults. They have no conception that their wails are an irritation. Toddlers do not spill their food, make messes, or whine because they want to drive mothers up the wall. That's just the way of toddlers. An abusive adult may have an unrealistic view of the way children should behave. The adult may feel a sense of personal failure if a child does not meet his or her unrealistic view of child behavior. The child then becomes "bad," and the adult doles out punishment.

The truth is that it's not the child's fault at all. Of course, children need to be disciplined in order to develop their own sense of right and wrong. But a spanking or a verbal reprimand is not the same as thrashing a child to the point of bruises, broken bones, and even death.

All parents have experienced exasperation and rage with their children's unacceptable behavior. The self-controlled adult will admit those feelings and take appropriate controlled action.

The uncontrolled adult will feel seized as if by an external force and harm the child. Some parents then feel deep remorse and guilt, if they sense that this kind of behavior does not fall under normal discipline. They may try to smooth things over and bribe the child into not telling anyone. The terrified child usually obeys because of dependence upon and fear of the parent. Any way that you look at this problem, it is an unhealthy situation.

Psychotherapy is indicated for anyone who feels he or she cannot control anger and feels impelled to take it out on children. Specially trained professionals can help an abusive parent, and without a condemning attitude. These professionals make every attempt to help the parent learn effective means of discharging rage. If you fear that you may be an abusive parent or stepparent, you can contact the American Humane Association for information and confidential referral:

> American Humane Association
> 5351 South Roslyn
> Englewood, Colorado 80110
> (303) 779-1400

Or you might contact the following organization:

Parents Anonymous
Dept. RB, Box F
2810 Artesia Blvd.
Redondo Beach, California 90278
(213) 371-3501

These organizations are under absolute mandate not to call the police. They are there to help you, not punish you.

What should you do if you suspect a parent of child abuse? Should you mind your own business? The answer lies in your response to this question: If you were a child whose parent kicked you, beat you to unconsciousness, or screamed at you for hours, would you want to be rescued?

The above-listed organizations help abusive parents by letting them know they are not the only persons with this particular problem. Many other community agencies are supposed to deal with child abuse; however, they vary widely in competency.

SELF-HELP GROUPS

Any common-interest group for stepparents will be helpful to you as a second parent. You could begin your own self-help group if no other competent resource exists in your community. The goal would be to share feelings about the job of stepparenting, to discuss solutions, and generally to decrease everyone's sense of being all alone in struggling with parenting responsibilities.

Beginning a group is simple. First, establish a meeting place. Many businesses have complimentary meeting rooms available in the evening. It is better to establish a meeting place outside the home for safety reasons, for one can fall prey to deranged types who attend home meetings just to evaluate possessions. The precaution of meeting in a neutral place relieves everyone of any worries about having strangers in the house.

Next, advertise in your local newspaper or over the local

radio or TV announcement service. Bulletin boards in community centers, churches, and clubs are excellent and inexpensive means of advertising. Include your telephone number in all publicity, so that you can get an idea of the number of people interested in attending.

Leaderless groups tend to drift apart, so someone must take the initiative during the first meeting. Strangers will be nervous about exposing their feelings to one another. If you have a large number of interested stepparents, try to break the crowd into groups of ten or fewer after the first meeting. Each cluster should have a guide who can easily talk about feelings and encourage reticent individuals to join in.

The best approach to relaxing people and getting them to verbalize feelings is to talk about yourself first. If you take the first step, casually giving your family's history, others will not be so threatened. You can also suggest arranging for speakers to come to discuss aspects of stepparenting with your group, just to prime the pump. Everyone will soon discover that sharing thoughts and feelings about one's unique role is fun, and will lighten the burden. After all, don't we all like to talk about ourselves?

One stepmother at such a group in our community related that she attended out of curiosity. She had thought that she had no problems with her family mix of four children. None of the kids seemed to display anger or resentment about her presence as a stepmother. However, after listening to others talk and question their roles, she realized she had been having negative feelings toward one of her stepdaughters. This eleven-year-old girl was revealing her anger in a very unusual way. She was *too* nice—was always neat, tidy, and helpful; was never late to the table; did not complain about anything (this is rare and unusual behavior in any child!); and was overly mannerly. If stepmother said, "Would you like some bacon," her stepdaughter would elaborately decline, "Oh, no, thank you; I wouldn't want you to cook that for me. Thank you very much, but I'm sure it's delicious." All this rhetoric over whether or not the kid wanted bacon!

During the group discussion it became obvious that the little girl was scared to act normally and had devised an act to cover up her true feelings. With the encouragement of the group, this stepparent came to view the situation for what it was. She also recognized that the child's constant correctness was grating on her serenity. All parents know that the perfectly behaved child is nonexistent. Our friend began to spend more time alone with her "little lady" stepdaughter. She slowly let the child know that it was "okay" to feel angry at her. Gradually their relationship deepened, and the stepdaughter resumed a normal pubescent life.

A stepfather brought up a problem he experienced with visitation rights. He said he felt deeply rejected when his stepson, at age sixteen, announced he wanted to live with his real father. "After ten years of my fathering and loving this boy, he up and leaves, and with the blessing of my wife!" This stepfather felt that his emotional investment was not appreciated by his stepson or his wife. It was normal for him to feel used and rejected. However, many boys, even before the teen years, would prefer to live with their Dads. In this situation, the mother understood her son's need and gave her approval.

Strict adherence to custody and visitation rights is a sign of parental rigidity. At certain stages of development it is healthy for boys to live with their fathers, if both so desire. The same emotional rule applies to daughters and mothers. If a child asks to live with one parent, the child's wishes should be given full consideration. The parent who is left behind should not lay guilt trips on the child, or feel rejected.

Remember that children are normally self-absorbed and do not think that adults experience rejection. If you give children freedom of choice, they will love and respect you for it in later years. If you try to hold on to them and to induce feelings of guilt or shame, they will hate you both in the present and in the future.

The rejected stepfather learned that his stepson's move was not directed against him personally. He grew by talking about his feelings and gaining insight about himself and his stepson. Their friendship was then given room to grow at some later time.

Whatever your feelings may be concerning your step-family, you can become an enriched person if you learn to communicate those feelings.

Chapter **12**

The Future Can *Be*
Beautiful

ALL PARENTING IS STRESSFUL

Whether one is a parent by choice, accident, or marriage, parenting is a heavy-duty responsibility. The stepparent's job is especially burdened because of the unnatural situation. The stepparent enters into children's lives with many strikes against successful relationships. The emotional hardships children experience from death or divorce will have left their invisible scars on their psyches.

We have discussed at great length how children carry the myth of the original family's reunion. The presence of a stepparent does little to disrupt this fantasy, no matter how kind and loving the "intruder" may be. Normal and abnormal jealousies must also be dealt with by both the adults and the children. Considering all of these extra stresses, it's a wonder that anyone is willing to become a second parent!

Special awards should be given to adults who survive the daily psychological stresses of stepparenting. Although natural parents often resent the normal lack of gratitude from their offspring, stepparents suffer even more. Where

137

are the rewards for taking on someone else's children? Certainly, there will be no thanks from the children themselves until later years.

In our society we are taught that a job well done will bring baubles and praise. Most adults, therefore, assume that if they do their best at parenting, the children will be appropriately thankful. Any parent knows from experience that this is often not the case.

The real rewards of successful parenting are otherwise. To know that you have done your best for a child's well-being adds to your own sense of accomplishment in life. Since all parents make mistakes in child rearing, do not berate yourself for your shortcomings.

Resiliency is one of the most amazing of human traits. Children can bounce back from trauma, neglect, and cruelty much more swiftly than adults. We've never really met a perfect parent, for there is no such person. Actually, we only have a vague notion of what that perfection may be.

GROWTH THROUGH LOVING

In any person's life there come times when priorities should be seriously questioned and sometimes rearranged in the service of true quality in living. Modern psychologists agree that a whole person is one who can love, work, and create to the best or his or her abilities. When this credo for successful living was formulated by Sigmund Freud, work had more significance than it does today. It was a time when craftsmanship, professionalism, and even parenting were held in high esteem. Today the majority of our population work for persons other than themselves. And most people are quick to admit that they find their jobs boring and unfulfilling. However, we all must work in order to survive and to make our small contributions to society. Since few of us will be remembered for any length of time for our accomplishments, working no longer does much for personal growth or high self-esteem.

This leaves us with love and creativity for giving us a sense of worth. Each person enters marriage with loving feelings and great hope for continued happiness. However, we have been reared in a society that values romantic love, but neglects to educate us to remain loving persons.

To have love in our life means that we must exert emotional effort every day to keep the love strong and enduring. To keep love alive and growing, we must tend to one another's needs. This attention is critical in any relationship, whether with friend, child, or mate. It takes creative thought to keep love a number-one priority.

We have seen many wealthy people in our years of practice. Although financial security brings materialistic pleasure, it does not guarantee happiness. The only truly serene and happy people we have known are those who know and understand the fact that loving relationships are the core of life. To live without loving and without being loved makes for a barren life. There are very few exceptions to this fact of life.

If your main relationship is a loving one, dealing with stepparenting will be so much easier. How do two adults, living in a hectic, highly stressful environment, maintain romance and creative love? It isn't easy, but it is definitely possible. Life should be fun and should have a large degree of carefreeness woven into its pattern. Little children view life with great curiosity and a joy of living. Too often this elan is squashed from their spirit, and thus they shelve the joy as a lost quality.

Realistically, the world of work is usually not an affectionate arena. The place where we seek and should enjoy love and affection is in our homes with family and friends. Two caring adults can make the home a haven from the emotional sterility of the outer world. If you and your mate are mutually willing to keep love alive, it will be the best legacy you can pass on to your children.

CHILDREN WILL LEAVE THE NEST

The thought probably seems quite distant, but all children become their own people eventually and move away from home. At that time, couples, particularly couples which include a stepparent, will have the freedom and privacy to grow even closer.

As a stepparent, you may find yourself more relieved by the children's leaving home than does the natural parent. Some parents become depressed when their offspring make the move for total independence. Unconsciously they don't really want their children to become adults. Women who have assumed the role of Supermom often feel useless when the children leave, realizing that they are no longer the most important figure in their children's lives. Such disappointment is the price one pays for investing one's self-esteem in parenting only. A husband's responsibility in this situation would be to encourage his wife to develop outside interests and to reveal to her how valuable she is to his life and happiness.

Parents who wish their children always to remain dependent upon them miss out on one of the great pleasures of parenthood—that their children can someday become their dearest friends. If the children are accepted as responsible and separate adults, they will respond with friendship. Friendship between an offspring and a parent is a very special and unique relationship. It's already a coupling that has intense bonding of some twenty years' duration, rich in experiences. That foundation, plus love, understanding, family feelings, and care can add immeasurably to everyone's life.

Gary, now twenty-five, considers his father and stepmother to be his best friends. It was not always this way. Gary was only seven when his parents divorced. When his father married Gwen, Gary suffered the usual jealousies and rejections that accompany divorce and remarriage. To compound his problems, his mother was a seductive woman who treated Gary as a replacement husband. She

continued to be in love with her ex and spent her days
labeling Gwen as a homewrecker. She effectively turned
Gary against his stepmother. He used to promise his neu-
rotic mother that when he grew up he would shoot his
stepmother and get Dad back again—a very unhealthy
state of mind for him.

Whenever Gary visited his father, which was frequently,
he tried to make life miserable for everyone. You can
imagine how betrayed he felt when his mother suddenly
remarried. She had set him up to disrupt his father's new
life by allowing him to think she still loved her ex. It took
several years of psychotherapy for Gary to work through
his resentments and anger. During those years he rebelled
by becoming a behavior problem in school, by drinking
excessively, and by frequently running away.

When Gary was suffering with his feelings, his stepmother was a consistent, supportive figure in his life. It
didn't occur to Gary how much time and effort Gwen had
expended on him, until he was away in the service. When
he returned to visit after his discharge, he sat down with
his father and stepmother and thanked them for their love
and patience. He also gained insight into his mother's
vengefulness and was able to forgive her, but not to like
her.

Gwen was a mature woman who knew that Gary and she
would eventually become friends if she gave him the understanding he needed. And it worked, adding enrich-
ment to both their lives.

If you keep the potential friendship in mind while you
are rearing children, you may find it easier to allow your
children to become autonomous. The ultimate goal of
parenting is to give children a sense of self-worth so that
they can become independent adults.

An independent adult is someone who can completely
take care of him- or herself. Whether male or female, a
mature person is able to manage a household. A mature
person can allow him- or herself to fall in love and to have

an adult, mutual dependency with another. A sense of humor is essential for a mature person. Responsibility, dependability, honesty, and compassion are all traits we equate with adulthood. These qualities are learned in the home from parents.

We also hope that our children will develop into adults who are thoughtful and who are expressive of their feelings. Such development can only occur if the children have received thoughtfulness and affection. As we mentioned in Part II, the infant's coping devices are quite limited. As parents and stepparents, we try to help children develop mature and workable coping skills for their future.

EVERY EVENT A GROWTH EXPERIENCE

As children grow, so should their parents; for all life experiences, positive and negative, can be growth experiences. Stepparenting definitely increases a person's flexibility, empathy, and understanding of the human condition. It also gives one a glimpse at one's personal resources and ability to care for someone else's children. You can take pride in the fact that no matter how tumultuous life becomes with stepchildren, you will have healed *some* of their original family wounds. Even if a stepchild never shows gratitude, some part of him or her will be thankful for your gifts of love and care. In passing this attitude on, you are preserving an ounce of human immortality.

Suggested Reading

Ainsworth, Mary Satter. *Deprivations of Maternal Care: A Reassessment of Its Effects.* Public Health Papers, No. 14. Geneva World Health Organization, 1962.

Bach, George and Peter Wyden. *The Intimate Enemy.* New York: William Morrow & Co., 1968.
An excellent book on how couples can argue, discuss, and fight in a fair manner.

Brody, Sylvia. *Patterns of Mothering: Maternal Influence During Infancy.* New York: International Universities Press, 1956.
Explains the profound effect that mothers have on their infants' sense of self.

Caine, Lynn. *Widow.* New York: William Morrow & Co., 1974.
A true experience of a widow. Mrs. Caine reports her personal journey through the mourning process.

Eiger, Marvin, M.D., and Sally Wendkasald. *The Complete Book of Breastfeeding.* New York: Workman Press, 1972.
Details the process of breastfeeding.

Erikson, Erik H. *Childhood and Society.* New York: W. W. Norton, 1950.
Explains the socialization process and how it affects a child's development.

Erikson, Erik H. *Growth and Crisis of the Healthy Personality.* Psychological Issues, Vol. 1, No. 1, Monograph No. 1. New York: International Press, 1959.
Relates how normal crises occur in human development and foster personality growth.

Gardner, Richard A. *The Boys and Girls Book about Divorce.* New York: Science House, 1970.
An excellent and readable book about the realities children must face during and after divorce. Meant to be read to children by parents. Highly recommended.

Goode, William. *After Divorce.* Glencoe, Illinois: Free Press, 1956.
Discusses what to expect of oneself after the trauma of divorce, and how to deal with practical and psychological problems that occur after divorce.

Grienstein, Alexander, M.D., and Edith Sterba, Ph.D. *Understanding Your Family.* New York: Random House, 1957.
A straightforward approach to family living, based on psychoanalytic principles but free of the jargon.

143

Horney, Karen. *Feminine Psychology.* In *New Ways of Psychoanalysis.* New York: W. W. Norton, 1939.
One of the intellectual leaders in the field of studying the unique qualities of women explains the female being.

Krantzler, Mel. *Creative Divorce.* New York: M. Evans & Co., 1974.
A beautiful book detailing how to end up friends instead of enemies after the divorce.

Lidz, Theodore, M.D. *The Person, His or Her Development Throughout the Life Cycle.* New York: Basic Books, 1968.
A textbook used in medical schools and psychoanalytic institutes for a complete understanding of human development. Extremely well written and highly recommended.

Lofas, Jeannette, and Ruth Roosevelt. *Living in Step.* New York: Stein & Day, 1976.
A sympathetic book with plenty of down-to-earth guidelines for step-families.

Maddox, Brenda. *The Half-Parent.* New York: M. Evans & Co., 1975.
A stepmother's personal experience, plus interviews with many other stepparents. A moving and helpful guide.

Mead, Margaret. *Male and Female.* New York: W. W. Norton, 1939.
A noted anthropologist looks at the basic differences and similarities between the male and female.

Ribble, Margaret A. *The Rights of Infants: Early Psychological Needs.* New York: Columbia University Press, 1943.
A comprehensive book exploring infantile needs beyond the physical ones.

Rosenbaum, Jean. *Becoming Yourself: The Teen Years.* Cincinnati: St. Anthony Messenger Press, 1970.
A book written for young teenagers to help them understand the adolescent process.

Rosenbaum, Jean. *The Mind Factor: How Your Emotions Affect Your Health.* New York: Prentice-Hall, 1972.
A book about psychosomatic illness and how stress creates disease.

Rosenbaum, Veryl. *Being Female: Discovering and Enjoying Your Physical, Emotional, and Sexual Nature.* New York: Prentice-Hall, 1973.
A book exploring the entire female person.

Salzman, Leon, M.D. *The Obsessive Personality.* New York: Science House, 1968.
An interesting treatment of individuals stuck in obsessive, repetitive thought and behavior patterns.

Spock, Benjamin, M.D. *Baby and Child Care.* Rev. ed. New York: Pocket Books, 1976.
A hit with new parents since first published. In this updated, revised edition Dr. Spock gives practical advice on every conceivable aspect of rearing children.

Spock, Benjamin, M.D. *Raising Children in a Difficult Time.* New York: W. W. Norton, 1974.

A book that covers many problems that occur in families and suggests how parents can cope with their children's needs.

Sullivan, Harry Stack. *The Interpersonal Theory of Psychiatry.* (1946-47.) Edited by Helen Perry and M. Gowel. New York: W. W. Norton, 1953.

This pioneer in the field of psychiatry explains how our personal interactions with others affect our growth.

U.S. Children's Bureau. *Your Child from One to Six.* Washington, D.C.: U.S. Government Printing Office, n.d.

A comprehensive look at children's physical and emotional development.

Winnicto, D. W. "Transitional Objects and Transitional Phenomena: A Study of the First Not-Me Possession." *International Journal of Psychoanalysis* 34 (1953): 89–97.

An explanation of how children can develop love relationships with objects or imaginary companions as they attempt to separate themselves from their mothers.